Math
for the
Very Young

Math for the Very Young

A Handbook of Activities for Parents and Teachers

Lydia Polonsky

Dorothy Freedman

Susan Lesher

Kate Morrison

Illustrated by Marcia Miller

John Wiley & Sons, Inc.

New York • Chichester • Brisbane • Toronto • Singapore

Copyright © 1995 by John Wiley & Sons, Inc.

"Feet," by Aileen Fisher, from Cricket in a Thicket, Scribner's, 1963, reprinted by permission of Aileen Fisher.

"Comma in the Sky" and "Old Man Moon," by Aileen Fisher, from In the Woods, in the Meadow, in the Sky, Scribner's, 1965, reprinted by permission of Aileen Fisher.

The publisher and the authors have made every reasonable effort to ensure that the experiments and activities in this book are safe when conducted as instructed but assume no responsibility for any damage caused or sustained while performing the experiments or activities in this book. Parents, guardians, and/or teachers should supervise young readers who undertake the experiments and activities in this book.

Library of Congress Cataloging-in-Publication Data

Math for the very young : a handbook of activities for parents and teachers /
   Lydia Polonsky... [et al.].
     p. cm.
     Includes bibliographical references and index
     ISBN 0-471-01671-3. — ISBN 0-471-01647-0 (paper)
     1. Mathematics—Study and teaching (Primary)   [1. Mathematical
   recreations.]   I. Polonsky, Lydia, 1950– .
   QA135.5.M36753   1995
   649'.68—dc20   94-20861

Printed in the United States of America
10 9 8 7 6 5 4 3 2

To our families

Contents

Chapter 4
Math on the Move 79

Chapter 5
Animal Facts and Figures 101

Chapter 6
Crafts That Use Math 119

Chapter 7
Games and Math 151

Chapter 8
Counting Rhymes and Stories 175

Index of Math Concepts 207

Foreword

The development of mathematical concepts and ways of thinking by young children begins well before they enter school. Their first years are spent exploring space and number through investigating their lives and environments. They learn that things fall, and that some things roll, but others don't. They learn about big and little. They learn about equal sharing as in "she has more than I do." They learn that it's better to ask for two cookies than one.

Unlike language development, however, this budding mathematical growth is often unnoticed by parents and caregivers, mainly because of the widespread belief that mathematics is something that can only be learned in school, and that if we're not writing numbers, we're not doing mathematics. This belief is far from true. Writing numbers comes last. First come ideas built from many experiences with the world and its objects. These are the foundations for strong mathematical intuitions that can, and should, be enhanced by parents and others who raise our children.

This book is a result of the collective knowledge, wisdom, and creativity of four superb classroom teachers who are colleagues of ours in the University of Chicago School Mathematics Project. In addition to their teaching, the authors have written mathematics curricular materials now being used in classrooms throughout the United States. The authors' understanding of children and the learning process has led to their belief that substantial bridges must be constructed to connect the formal mathematics taught in schools with the informal mathematics present in the child's environment.

Thus, they have given us a lively, practical guide to nurturing mathematics in young children. Their premise is that there are numerous opportunities to help children explore the mathematics in everyday activities and that there is no need to do or buy anything "special." They have written a book that helps both adults and children see that mathematics is everywhere, that it is useful, and that it is fun.

Sheila Sconiers and Max Bell
The University of Chicago School Mathematics Project

Introduction

Ideas about how children learn mathematics have changed dramatically from the days of the old memorize-and-drill system by which many of us were taught. It is now understood that young children can think about complex mathematical ideas long before they are able to deal with symbolic written work. Not only are children far more intuitive in their mathematical thinking than educators formerly realized, but the need for all children to be at home in the world of mathematics in an increasingly technological age is more pressing than ever before.

LEARNING MATH EVERY DAY

We have taught in classrooms for many years. We also have written math curricula for young children for the University of Chicago School Mathematics Project as well as for our own classrooms. In our classrooms, math is a part of our everyday routines—measuring and recording the temperature, keeping track of the number of days the children are in school, marking dates on the calendar, counting, estimating, and asking questions such as "Is there a pattern here?" We measure sizes and weights. We organize crackers at snack time into orderly rows and columns. Many of our games and craft activities use mathematical ideas.

These activities lead to mathematical discussions that are part of the ordinary discourse of the day. The children grow comfortable with these ideas and learn to think about mathematical relationships in very natural ways. They become problem solvers, not rote learners.

In writing this handbook for young children who are learning mathematics, we have followed this approach. We feel certain that as you become aware of the possibilities for thinking and talking and doing math in a relaxed way, you will be delighted with your child's ability to grow into an interested and flexible math thinker.

MATH CONCEPTS IN THIS BOOK

The mathematical ideas included in this book fall into five general areas: pattern, number, collecting and understanding data, geometry, and measurement.

Pattern

When children explore a pattern, they are solving problems—analyzing the rules that govern the pattern and extending the pattern by following those rules. In communicating their discoveries, they are developing both their language skills and math concepts. They are learning to find connections and make predictions, and to look for similarities and differences. In this handbook, children will find patterns in nature as they examine the markings of animals at the zoo and in the wind and tide marks at the beach, and make rubbings of leaves. They will create patterns with real objects as they manipulate colored pieces of cereal to make a necklace, or cover a surface with a repeated shape to make a tessellation. They will explore the patterns of symmetry while making snowflakes, paper dolls, and "stained glass windows." And they will also begin to do some patterning using the letters of their names.

Number

From early infancy, children begin developing ideas of number. When eating cookies, they recognize whether they have more or less than someone else. Such simple activities as collecting pebbles at the beach, sharing a treat with friends, and blowing out candles on a birthday cake are first experiences with adding, subtracting, and dividing.

Children's early number experiences also include learning to count. This is a very pleasurable activity for most children. They enjoy counting rhymes, chants, and beats. As they put a number sequence together and grow comfortable counting forward and backward, they become aware of the patterns and relationships that make up our number system.

Children also need experiences counting objects. In the activities in this book, children can count the number of people in their families, the number of legs on a spider, and the number of cards dealt out in a game of Go Fish. All these activities lead to ideas of comparison between numbers.

Before children write numbers, they learn to recognize them as they change the TV channel, set a timer, or make a telephone call. They will have opportunities to write numbers through recording height and weight and other personal data.

Collecting and Understanding Data

In this complex world, we must learn to deal with an overwhelming amount of information coming at us electronically, on paper, and through verbal communication. We need the skills to sort through this information and make meaningful decisions about it.

This book suggests ways to help children handle data that is meaningful to them. They will collect important numbers, from addresses and phone numbers to height, weight, and shoe size. They will take linear measurements using parts of their bodies and various instruments, such as rulers and tape measures. Children learn to record this data in a variety of ways, making charts and scrapbooks and constructing graphs. Talk with your child about the data that is discovered through these activities. It is this communication, above all else, that helps children take meaning from the information that surrounds them.

Geometry

All children explore their surroundings and, in doing so, collect a great variety of information about the objects that make up their world. This book contains activities that encourage further exploration.

Children look for and identify two- and three-dimensional shapes on walks around the neighborhood or rides in the family car. They will add to their store of positional terms, such as high, low, over and under, whether they are romping at the local playground or sitting quietly working on a simple weaving. They will manipulate shapes by playing with marshmallows and toothpicks or a set of tangrams.

These explorations make children increasingly aware of the different properties of familiar objects and their relationship to one another.

Measurement

Young children begin to learn about measurement through their experiences in the everyday world. Play with water and sand, in which children pour from one container to another, is an opportunity to experience measures of volume and make informal comparisons. Cooking presents many opportunities to learn about volume, temperature, and time measurement. Making a garden is a natural way to learn something about linear measurement through planting seeds at the appropriate depth and distance apart.

Many times measurement experiences are approximate, as in choosing the pan in which to bake a chicken (and discussing the reasons for the choice). At other times, the activities involve using standard measures, as in baking a cake.

All these experiences contribute to the growth of understanding ideas of measurement in young children.

HOW TO USE THIS BOOK

Rather than organize this book by mathematical concept, we have organized it around events and happenings of family life. If you are looking for activities that focus on a particular concept, refer to the Index of Math Concepts at the back of the book. We hope that you and your child will begin to enjoy the pleasure of doing math together as you now enjoy telling stories and reading books. Once you become familiar with some of the ideas, we hope you will feel free to expand on our examples and make up your own activities. You will undoubtedly recognize some things that you already do with your child. Many activities use common household items, but feel free to substitute or improvise. Our purpose is to help you focus on math that is inherent in our daily lives.

We suggest that this book be approached in a playful, easy-going manner. These are not lessons to be learned. There is no predetermined order. This book can be used over a period of many years. Some activities are appropriate for very young children, while others provide a challenge for somewhat older children. There is no prescribed amount of time, either by day or by week. Follow your child's interests. Let mutual enjoyment be your guide.

Chapter 1

Math Around the House

Mathematical comprehension and skills are nurtured through a rich variety of real-life experiences. There are many opportunities in daily life to enhance a young child's interest in and understanding of mathematical ideas.

Not only are there mathematical rewards for children who help around the house, but there are personal rewards as well. Children's feelings of self-esteem are nourished when they feel they are important, contributing members of the family. In a pleasant, nonpressured, cooperative atmosphere, much worthwhile learning can take place.

COOKING

Young children relish a chance to help cook. They love to feel helpful and to handle the exciting grown-up tools of the trade. Cooking is full of mathematical possibilities. Here are some important mathematical concepts you can introduce to your child while you are cooking together.

Measuring   Cooking provides an excellent opportunity to begin to learn about the sizes of standard measuring cups and spoons and about how to handle and use them. It is also a natural and practical place to introduce the idea and language of fractions.

Estimating   You are trying to estimate a measurement when you say, "How big a pan do we need to roast this chicken?" Your child can help with this decision by comparing the chicken to several different pans and helping

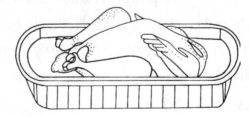

Which pan would be the best fit?

select the one that is the best fit. You are also trying to estimate when you say, "How many beans do we need for the three of us?"

Temperature   Setting the oven temperature for baking is a good chance to use big numbers in a useful way. The more familiar a variety of numbers becomes in real-life situations, the more meaningful they will be.

If you use an oven, meat, or candy thermometer or keep a thermometer in the refrigerator or freezer, you can help your child become familiar with these various tools for reading temperature and with the different functions they perform.

Time   Your child can help to time your cooking project. You can use a timer, or you can help a non–clock reader watch for the finish time by giving clues about where the clock hands will be on an analog (standard) clock. If you are using a digital clock, you can point out that there are two different numbers separated by a colon. The first number gives the hour, and the second describes minutes after the hour.

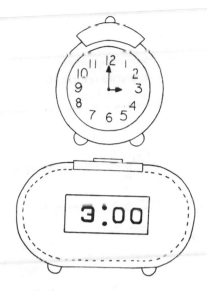

Shapes and Patterns   Your young cook will enjoy taking a small bit of biscuit or cookie dough and rolling it into a snake, then coiling the snake into different designs and shapes. Make standard geometric shapes, such as squares, triangles, and circles, or experiment with shapes that curve into wiggly lines, faces, or animals. You can also roll out the dough with a rolling pin. Use different shaped cookie cutters to form numbers, letters, animals, hearts, and any shape that appeals to the cooks in your family.

Both of these clocks tell you it is three o'clock.

Arrays   When you put cookies or biscuits on a baking pan, arrange them in orderly rows and columns. This sort of regular arrangement, called an array, is one example of a multiplication pattern and helps lay the groundwork for ideas of multiplication. For example, a 3-by-4 array has 12 members. There are 3 rows with 4 items in each row, which makes 12 items altogether ($3 \times 4 = 12$).

Show your child how to count the number of cookies arranged on the baking sheet. It is interesting to compare how much easier it is to count the total number of cookies placed in an array than to count cookies put down at random.

You are making an array when you put your cookies on the baking sheet in orderly rows and columns.

MAKING SCONES

Try this recipe for scones, a delicious, biscuitlike tea cake. *Scone* may be pronounced to rhyme with either *flown* or *gone*. In any case, they don't last long, and there is much mathematics in the making.

While helping you with this recipe, your child will learn about measuring, experimenting with volume, timing, working with circles and triangles, setting the temperature for the oven, and using simple fractions.

Ingredients	2	cups flour	5	tablespoons butter or margarine
	2	tablespoons sugar	½	cup currants or raisins (optional)
	3	teaspoons baking powder	1	egg
	½	teaspoon salt		about ¾ cup milk

---

1. Preheat oven to 425°F.

2. Measure the flour, sugar, baking powder, and salt. Mix these dry ingredients together in a large bowl. Using a pastry blender or two knives, cut in the butter or margarine until the pieces of butter are the size of small peas. Stir in currants or raisins, if desired.

3. In a measuring cup, lightly beat the egg. Add enough milk to the egg to measure a total of ¾ cup. Add this to the mixture of dry ingredients and butter, and stir quickly, just until the ingredients form a slightly sticky, soft ball of dough.

4. Turn the dough onto a floured board and knead very lightly about ten times. Form the dough into two balls. Flatten each ball with the palm of your hand until the circles are about ½ inch thick.

5. Cut one circle into 6 triangular wedges, the other into eight. Which are larger—the scones that are ⅙ of a circle or those that are ⅛ of a circle?

6. Place the triangular wedges on a greased cookie sheet so that their sides are not touching.

7. Bake until golden brown. Eat immediately with butter or margarine, and jam or honey. How long do they last in your home?

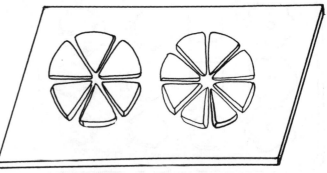

One ball of dough has been cut into six pieces and the other into eight pieces. Which pieces are bigger, the sixths or the eighths?

Shape Meals

To familiarize your child with some basic shapes, plan a meal together in which one shape is used throughout. Making choices and sharing ideas with your child is an important part of the activity. Here are a few of the possibilities:

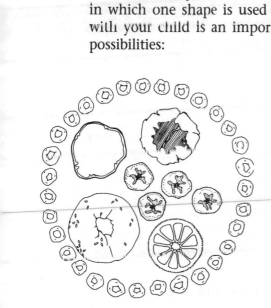

Circles for Breakfast

orange and banana slices
Cheerios
pancakes
English muffins
bagels

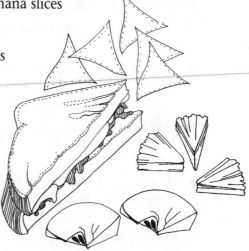

Triangles for Lunch

peanut butter and jelly sandwich
tortilla chips
apple and pineapple wedges
scones

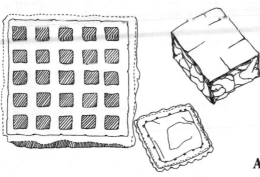

A Square Meal

meatloaf
lasagna
ravioli
crackers and cheese
brownies
waffles

Food Counts

Working with food presents lots of good opportunities for counting and estimating. Practicing counting helps to build familiarity with and understanding
of our number system. There are many occasions, however, when knowing
what is "about the right amount" is more practical and useful than doing an
actual count. Therefore, being a good estimator is a useful skill as well as a way
of helping to develop good "number sense."

COUNTING AND ESTIMATING

* Empty a small bag of M&Ms onto a table. Without counting, guess how
  many there are all together, then count them.

* Without counting, guess which color of M&Ms has the most pieces?
  Which color has the fewest pieces? Sort them by color and count to find
  out. Check another bag of M&Ms . Does it follow the same pattern of dis-
  tribution, or is it different?

* Count the segments of an orange. Do all oranges have the same number
  of segments?

* Count out 20 unshelled peanuts. Guess how many nuts are inside them.
  Open the shells and count to find out.

WEIGHING AND ESTIMATING

* Describe the difference between spinning a raw egg and spinning a hard-
  boiled egg. Which do you think weighs more, a hard-boiled egg or a raw
  egg?

* Does popcorn weigh more popped or unpopped?

FRUIT FRACTIONS

Cut an apple into halves, quarters, and eighths. You can do this through the
poles or the equator. How would you divide a banana into halves, quarters,
and eighths?

WASHING DISHES

Even dishwashing can have its mathematical moments. For starters, as noted in the following poem, there are opportunities to sort, subtract, measure and count. Add some lines of your own to help speed up the work.

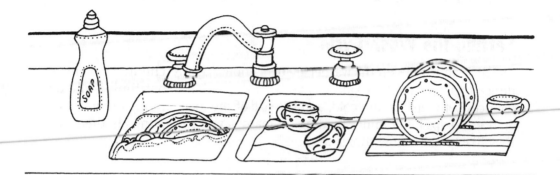

DOING DISHES

There's not much good to say about the dishes.
Cats don't do them nor do fishes.
Clean them up nice and bright
They'll still be back tomorrow night.
But math is there if you're alert
Sorting spoons, subtracting dirt
Measure soap, add some water
Get to work both son and daughter.
Work together husbands, wives
Don't forget to count the knives.
Though dishes seem to multiply
Dividing work will make time fly.

—Dorothy Freedman

DOING LAUNDRY

You may wonder, what does the laundry have to do with mathematics?

There are the tasks of measuring the washing powder or liquid, estimating the amount of clothes that can fill, but not overfill, the washing machine, and the important mathematical task of relating or sorting things.

Setting the Wash Cycle

The dials and knobs on the washer are mysterious to most children but are not difficult to explain. This kind of hands-on discussion about timing, the differences between hot and cold, and the size of the load, among other considerations, helps build understanding on many levels for young children. And they like to know how things work.

Sorting the Clothes

The rules for sorting the laundry call for decisions about how different clothes relate to and differ from each other. These relationships are primarily by temperature (hot, warm, cold) and by color (white, light colors, dark colors), and perhaps also by person, especially if there is a baby in the family whose clothes require a gentler detergent.

Sorting the laundry

Putting the Clothes Away

Sorting and putting the clothes away after they have been washed and dried involves making many distinctions that have mathematical implications.

Here are a few examples:

Size   Is it big or little or somewhere in between?

Color and Pattern   Are there matching pieces that need to be put together?

Ownership   Do these socks belong to Bart, Matt, Josh, or Tom—or Johanna?

Pairs   Is there only one sock when there should be two (a not uncommon problem)?

Function   Will this towel be used in the kitchen or the bathroom?

The ability to see relationships and distinctions—the things that belong together and those which do not—lays a foundation for the mathematical ideas of properties and attributes that underlie these decisions. The laundry can be a good laboratory for the young mathematician to explore.

KEEPING TIME

HOW MANY SECONDS IN A MINUTE?

How many seconds in a minute?
Sixty, and no more in it.

How many minutes in an hour?
Sixty for sun and shower.

How many hours in a day?
Twenty-four for work and play.

How many days in a week?
Seven both to hear and speak.

How many weeks in a month?
Four, as swift as the moon runn'th.

How many months in a year?
Twelve the almanac makes clear.

How many years in an age?
One hundred says the sage.

How many ages in time?
No one knows the rhyme.

—Christina G. Rossetti

As far back as we can look, people have been interested in keeping time. The sun, moon, stars, seasons, and day and night, in their regular changes, have been watched and kept track of. From birth, infants begin the rhythms of sleep and wakefulness, hunger and fullness.

But modern people divide time into much smaller units than primitive people, and children, even at an early age, are governed by units of hours and minutes, and sometimes even seconds. We surround ourselves with implements for telling time: calendars, watches, clocks, timers.

An understanding of the units of time builds slowly in children, as they link the terms to events in their own lives that have meaning for them. This awareness, like all early mathematical learning, builds upon having experiences in the real world and then thinking and talking about those experiences.

"Patsch-Clapping" Time

What does it mean when people say "Wait a second" or "I'll only be a minute"? You can count seconds and minutes quite accurately using "patsch-claps" to help you keep up a steady rhythm.

This is how to patsch-clap. To "patsch," bring your hands down to slap the front of your thighs. Then clap by bringing your hands together. Each patsch-clap takes about 1 second. "Patsch-clap, Patsch-clap, Patsch-clap," is 3 seconds.

There are 60 seconds in a minute—try to patsch-clap together for 1 minute. If you patsch-clapped for a full hour, the hour would seem very long indeed. An hour is 60 minutes, or 3,600 seconds, or 3,600 patsch-claps.

Using "patsch-clapping" to count a minute without a clock

Clocks

Children become familiar with phrases like "We have to leave in ten minutes" and "We'll have dinner in half an hour," and begin to build up an inner sense of these units of time. Learning to read a digital clock is a much simpler task than learning to tell time on a standard, or analog, clock, but many children don't feel they have learned to tell time until they can decode the meaning of a "real" clock. It may be helpful for adults to realize some of the difficulties inherent in learning this task.

The analog clock is a land mine of seeming contradictions. The same set of numbers stands for the units of both hours and minutes; and the long hand points out the shorter units of time (minutes), while the short hand points out the longer units (hours). Though the numbers on the clock represent hours, which is a 1-to-12 count, when the minute hand is in those positions, it is counting a series of 1 to 60.

So go slowly in teaching children to tell time on an analog clock! When your child expresses an interest, concentrate at first only on the positions of the hour hand, including not only when it points directly to the hour but also when it's "almost at the 3" or "about halfway between the 5 and the 6." When you introduce the minute hand, stick to the "o'clocks" at first. Be prepared to stop as soon as you sense confusion setting in.

You might consider getting your child a clock or wristwatch. There are many reasonably priced ones available. Owning a clock or wristwatch while learning to tell time can give a child a sense of pride and accomplishment.

The following activities can help your child become familiar with clocks and with units of time.

Time for Television Turning on the television for a favorite show can be your young viewer's job. You can give a simple clue such as "It will be six o'clock when the short hand is pointing straight down at the 6 and the long hand is pointing straight up, where the 12 is."

Beat the Clock If your child is inclined to dawdle in the morning when it's time to get dressed, you might play "Beat the Clock." Besides helping your child to get dressed with dispatch, it will help develop a sense of the passage of time. You can give simple clues about where the hands of the clock will be by the time the child should have finished dressing.

Children can also time themselves with a kitchen timer. Kitchen timers are relatively easy to set, and children can learn to read numbers, including the confusing teens, if they have experience setting these times. If you use a timer to play "Beat the Clock," agree on a reasonable amount of time in which to get dressed, and let your child set the timer. Your kitchen helper can also set the timer when you are cooking, and will begin to develop a sense of time in this way.

PLANNING PARTIES

No celebration of number can match the arrival of a birthday. Planning for a party to celebrate the day can provide lots of mathematic opportunities.

How Many Candles?

Together, you and your child can count out the candles, one for each year the birthday child has reached, with perhaps "one more to grow on." If the birthday celebrant doesn't manage to blow out all the candles at the first try, at least there is a subtraction problem! How many candles are left?

How Many Guests?

How many guests can be invited? This is usually also a moment when negotiations for more or fewer are carried out. It is a chance to discuss reasons such as space, time, and expense (and often, energy) that influence how many friends can be invited.

Invitations

Even young children can help add something to the invitations—put on stamps, and mail the cards in a mailbox or at a post office. You can encourage them to figure out how many stamps will be needed and to think about how many days before the party to mail the invitations. The more concrete experiences they have and the more they are able to help, the more responsible they will feel and the more they will learn.

Setting Up

Helping set the table at regular meals is good experience in mastering one-to-one correspondence (one person/one fork), and counting out plates and silverware for the party guests is good practice in practical counting.

The Cake

If the birthday cake is homemade, let your child help with the baking and decorating. It's a chance to put measuring and timing to good use.

Prizes and Favors

If guests are to be given prizes or favors, the birthday child can help choose them. Agree together ahead of time on a price range, and stay reasonably close to it. If you decide how much you will spend on each guest, and there are to be six guests, you can work out the total budget together on the calculator. (See the discussion of calculator use later in this chapter.) When you get to the store, you will already have a working figure to operate within that makes sense to both of you, and your child will have had a valuable mathematical experience with numbers and money. (See "The Grocery Store " in chapter 4 for a more detailed account of money.)

Buying Presents

When children are guests at a birthday party, it is good to let them be involved in selecting the present within an agreed-upon price range. If possible, use this opportunity to let them handle money, paying for the gift and receiving the change.

Wrapping Presents

Wrapping the present is a good opportunity for more math thinking. Experienced present wrappers estimate the amount of paper necessary for the job quite accurately. Wrappers new to the job need to assess the amount by experimentally draping the paper around the package to get a close approximation of the paper needed. It is a good lesson in adapting a flat surface (the paper) to a three-dimensional object (the present). Another good puzzler: How much ribbon will you need to wrap the present?

Estimating how much paper is needed to wrap the gift

COLLECTING THINGS

SORTING AND COUNTING

Look for math and you will find it
For example, in collecting
When you decide what to include
You'll find you are selecting.

Put it in order, look for patterns
Watch your collection mount
And as it grows don't you suppose
It will lead to an excellent count?

—Dorothy Freedman

Children seem to be natural collectors. They collect dolls and beetles, baseball cards and stamps, dollhouse furniture, rocks and seashells, and whatever else interests them.

While thinking about their collections and playing with them, children form categories by size, shape, date, point of origin, function, design, or other appropriate attributes, all of which are mathematical forms of thought. As their collections grow, they will begin to count to higher and higher numbers.

If your child doesn't have a collection yet, look for things that might be of interest. It might be coins or rocks or model airplanes or toy horses —whatever appeals to your young mathematician.

Collecting can be rewarding. It helps teach about classification and meaningful counts.

READING MAPS

Hang a large map, the bigger the better, in a room in your house where your family spends a lot of time—the kitchen, dining room, den, or TV room, for example. You could have a large map of the world as well as ones of the United States, your state, and your city or town.

The idea is to make the map a familiar presence that can be easily referred to during family discussions. You can point out places that are mentioned in the news as well as places you and friends have traveled. Besides helping to orient your child in the world, referring to maps leads to plenty of math talk.

Map Math Talk

Use words that describe direction:
- north (the top of the map)
- south (the bottom of the map)
- east (the right-hand side of the map)
- west (the left-hand side of the map)

Make a point of using words that describe relative distances:
- far, farther, farthest ("Who lives farther away, Luke or Sam?")
- near, nearer, nearest

Try estimating the number of miles traveled ("About how far is it to Grandma's?"). You can use a road map to figure out the actual miles traveled. Discuss time, distance, and speed. ("About how long will it take if we fly? Or drive? Or go by train? Which will be fastest?").

Family Travels

Your child can get an idea of where distant family members live if you mark those places on a map with colored tacks or stickers. You can also keep a record of the places that your family travels using this method. Put the markers on your big wall map, or draw up a special family map that shows the route you take to the beach, to school, to Grandmother's house, or other favorite places.

GROWING PLANTS

Growing plants from seed can be both a mathematical and a horticultural experience.

Getting Started

Check out the site you have chosen for a few days before you plant to see if it is in full sun, partial shade, or deep shade. Once you and your child have studied the light conditions that will be available for your plants, you can decide together what kind of plants will do best in these conditions—for example, beans, peas, lettuce, or zinnias, marigolds, or impatiens. Choose plants that appeal to your young gardener and can flourish in your growing conditions.

Measuring

After preparing the soil together according to instructions on the seed packet, you and your child can measure your plot. Next, stretch a string (which, of course, you measure, too!) between two sticks to make a straight guideline for marking the row to be planted.

Check the seed packet to find the suggested planting depth and distance between plants. Mathematical terms take on meaning when you use them to describe real situations, so encourage using words that describe location: *near, far, deep, shallow, in, over, above,* and *below.*

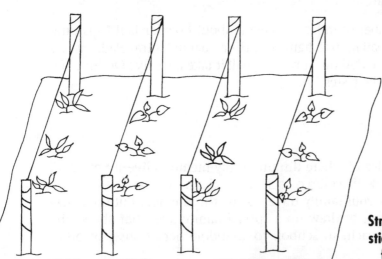

Strings stretched between two sticks make straight guidelines for the rows of your plot.

Standard Measures or Estimates?

You can use a standard measuring tool, such as a ruler, yardstick (meter stick), or tape measure, to measure the distance between seeds and the depth at which to plant them, or you can estimate. You can also try finger-and-arm measuring: on an adult, the first joint of the index finger is about 1 inch, the width of the little fingernail is about 1 centimeter, and the distance between outstretched arms is about 1 yard (1m). Let your child use you as a ruler.

A Rule of Thumb

The bigger the seed, the deeper it should be planted; the smaller the seed, the shallower. Understanding the relationship between the size of the seed to be planted and the depth of the hole to be dug uses the concept of ratio, or the relation of one thing to another.

Watching Them Grow

There is a good opportunity for a meaningful count if your young gardener keeps track of the days it takes the seeds to sprout by marking off the days on the calendar. When the plants begin to grow, try measuring them from time to time.

COUNTING ON CALCULATORS

Calculators make wonderful gifts for children, and there are many reasonably priced ones on the market. Solar powered calculators don't require batteries

Types of Calculators

There are two basic types of calculators. One type, designed especially for children, uses beeps or flashing symbols to give clues about correct answers. The standard calculator is also very rewarding for young children to play and experiment with. These ordinary calculators offer the opportunity for open-ended exploration and discovery without worrying about wrong answers.

Simple Explanations

When using calculators, it's a good idea not to overwhelm young children with lengthy explanations or to try to give answers to questions they haven't asked. In general, it's best to keep answers simple and to the point. Encourage a playful approach so that your child feels free to experiment and make up games. (Some children pretend their calculators are telephones and "call" each other up, punching in their real phone numbers on their calculators.) Try to keep the feeling open-ended and experimental, with the child in charge of the experience and you giving information only as requested.

Two Helpful Keys

C IS FOR CLEAR

The C key is very helpful. It erases old work and lets you go on to new things.

THE = KEY

The = key has two important uses:

- It can be used to complete a number sentence: 1 + 3 = 4
- On most calculators it can also be used as a repeat key:

To count by ones, press the + key, the 1 key, and then the – key to set the pattern for adding one more. After that, each time you press the = key, the calculator will continue to add one more. You are counting by ones!

To count by fives or any other number, follow the same procedure, using + 5 = or the number you wish to count by.

This is a fascinating way to experiment with skip counting (counting by numbers other than one). Besides presenting number patterns that are interesting in themselves, skip counting will prove very helpful when it comes time to learn multiplication facts.

Calculator Stories

Your young mathematician can practice using numbers by playing story answer games. For example, say to your child, "There was Father Bear, and Mother Bear, and wee little Baby Bear. Can you show me on the calculator how many bears there were?" Then let your child find numeral 3 on the calculator and press the key to give the answer. You can take turns telling a story and giving calculator answers.

Telephone Number and Home Address

The calculator is a good place to practice writing the child's home phone number, including area code. It also provides a way to practice writing the child's home address, including street and apartment numbers, if any. It's important for children to have this information. Using a calculator is also a good way for them to get used to reading big numbers that have some relevance to their lives.

Chapter 2

Growing and Changing: Making a Personal Record Book

"Tell me about when I was born."
"Show me my baby pictures."
"What were you like when you were little?"
"I'm much bigger now than when I was a baby."
"Will I always be the smallest?"

All children ask questions like these because they are intensely interested in their family histories and personal growth. Children ask for confirmation that they are growing up and are no longer babies. A family photo album provides hours of entertainment and learning as children hear stories of their family and see their own growth and change recorded in pictures. Helping your child collect, discuss, and record personal data and information can link this natural interest to mathematical understanding.

You and your child can shop together for a special notebook to serve as the child's personal growth record and memory book. A scrapbook with large, blank pages is ideal.

You will probably do most or all of the writing as you discuss the various entries with your child. Children love to dictate and see their words written down. Your young artist can illustrate the book and draw symbols for data that are to be recorded. The child can also choose the photos that are to be included.

The following sections provide examples of pages that could be included in your child's personal record book.

**Use a photograph or self-portrait of your child on the first page
of the personal record book.**

USEFUL NUMBERS TO KNOW

My name is Katie Smith

Other
important
numbers

I Live at
345 Lincoln Ave.
Chicago, Illinois
60610

My phone
number
(312) 555-4326

_____
_____
_____

Help your child write your family's important numbers.

It is important for children to learn their addresses and telephone numbers, including area codes. Set aside a page for your child to practice writing these numbers. This is good math practice as well as an important safety precaution.

Help your child learn the placement of the numbers on the telephone. Take time with your child to practice dialing your home number as well as 911, the emergency number, and 0 (zero), to contact the operator.

ALL ABOUT THE FAMILY

Your child's self-made portraits and photos of family members and special people may take several pages of the record book. You may want to include the ages of the people in the pictures. Help your child find groups or sets among the members of your family, such as:

- males, boys, or men
- females, girls, or women
- brown-eyed people, blue-eyed people, etc.
- brunettes, blondes, etc.
- tall people, short people, etc.
- people who wear glasses
- pets

You will find many more groupings within your own extended family. Your child can count the members of each group. Encourage your child to see that family members fit more than one group. For instance, Aunt Sue is a female, wears glasses, and is blonde.

Mom   Dad   Me   Tommy

Grandma   Grandpa   Aunt Sue   Rover

Collect family photos.

You can also play a family guessing game. One player might say, "I'm thinking of a person in our family who is tall and wears glasses." The other player responds with an answer. Playing with grouping and sorting is important practice and develops mathematical thinking.

An excellent commercial game that uses this same idea is Guess Who? The Mystery Face Game, by Milton Bradley Company.

BODY MEASUREMENTS—FROM TOP TO TOE

Height

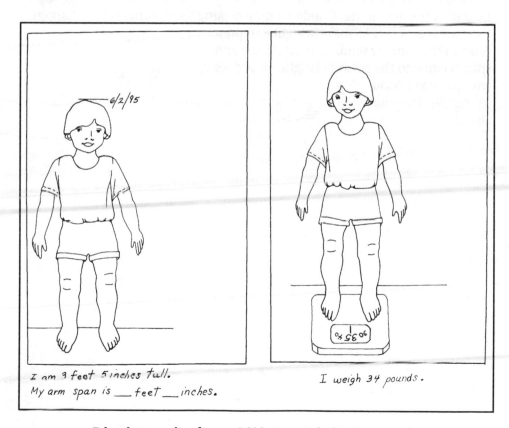

I am 3 feet 5 inches tall.
My arm span is ___ feet ___ inches.

I weigh 34 pounds.

Take photographs of your child being weighed and measured.

Have your child stand against a wall or doorjamb. Mark his or her height with a ruler and pencil, and write the date next to the mark. Then, measure from the floor to the pencil mark. Your child will enjoy helping you do this. Take a photo of your child being measured, and add it to the record book.

You may even want to devote one wall or doorjamb of your home to family height measurements taken over the years. Children love comparing their present height to the previous marks and seeing a physical representation of their growth and change. The wall will get marked, but the permanent gallery of your children's growing years will be precious. If you use indelible ink, the wall can be washed without removing the marks.

Your child will also enjoy measuring favorite dolls and stuffed animals. You may want to record on an additional scrapbook page the lengths or heights of family pets—though it will take patience and several pairs of hands!

Measure your child's arm span while he or she lies faceup. If this is done in sand or snow, your child can make a body impression and then get up to help with the measuring. Children enjoy making "snow angels" by "flapping" their arms and legs to make winglike impressions in the snow or sand. In an adult, the arm span is equal to the person's height. How does arm span correspond to height in your child?

Is your child's arm span equal to his or her height?

Weight

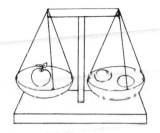

"Look, my apple weighs as much as two eggs!"

Children love weighing themselves. Show them how to stand on the scale and find the number that represents their weight. Take a photo of your child being weighed, and place it in the record book.

Children also enjoy weighing toys and various household articles. For light objects, use a kitchen scale. Balance scales don't show weight but are useful for comparing weights of various objects. Such scales are available in stores and are fun for children to use. Help your child place objects on each pan of the scale and see whether they balance. If they do, then the objects are equal in weight. Your child will discover that the lower pan contains objects that weigh more than those in the higher pan. Children enjoy putting things in and taking things out of the pans as they make discoveries and predictions about weights.

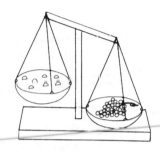

"How many more gumdrops should I add to balance the grapes?"

Height and Weight over Time

Watch Me Grow!

Date	Height	Weight
June 2, 1995	3 feet 5 inches	34 pounds

Organize and record your child's growth with a simple chart.

You may want to devote one scrapbook page to a simple height and weight record of your child. The two of you can decide how often to update the record. It could be monthly, quarterly, or as often as seems right for your child's interest. This project is a first step in learning to organize and record numbers.

An interesting fact to tell your child is that most people, both children and adults, shrink approximately 1 inch (2.5 cm) during the course of the day. This is due to the forces of gravity working on our bodies. We regain the height during our nightly sleep. To prove this, measure your child's height in the morning and then again before bedtime. Astronauts in space, released from the pull of Earth's gravity, have been found to temporarily increase their height by as much as 2 inches (5 cm).

Another way to help your child keep track of height and weight changes is to introduce a simple bar graph. Graphs are mathematical drawings that illustrate a relationship between sets of data. Start your child's bar graph by drawing the axes of the graph—dates across the bottom and measurements

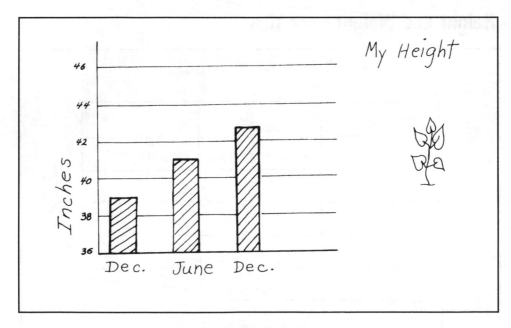

**Use a bar chart to provide a graphic picture of
your child's growth over time.**

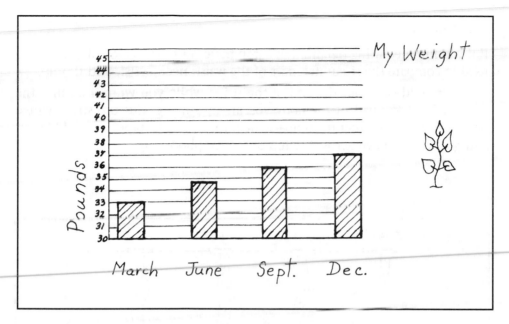

A bar chart of your child's weight over time

in a column on the left—on the scrapbook page. Then, extend the measurement guidelines across the page. Your child can then find his or her height and weight in the column of numbers at the left and draw a color bar above the appropriate month.

Discuss with your child the change or lack of change from month to month. There may be gradual change or a lack of growth for a time, followed by a sudden growth spurt. This is natural. It is important for your child to understand that growth is a very individual thing. No two people grow at exactly the same rate. However a child grows is right for that child.

Circumference

If it was fun measuring height, don't stop there. Yarn, string, or ribbon can be used to compare the circumferences of the waist, neck, wrist, and thumb.

Your child can hold the end of the string while you wrap it around the wrist or whatever part of the body you are measuring. Cut the string where both ends meet. In order to compare the measurements, tape one end of each string to a line drawn across the top of the scrapbook page.

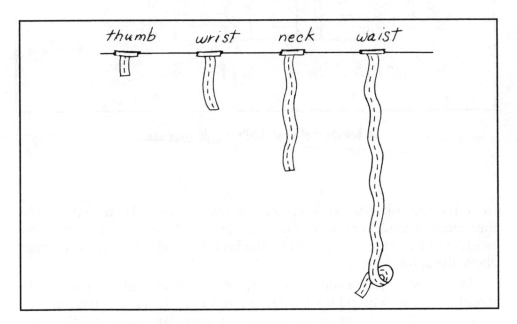

"My waist is eight times bigger around than my thumb!"

It is interesting to discover that the circumference of the wrist is about twice that of the thumb; the circumference of the neck is about twice that of the wrist; and the circumference of the waist is about twice that of the neck. Remember, as with height and weight, these ratios are just approximations.

Feet

Help your child trace his or her bare foot and shoe on a scrapbook page. To make an accurate measurement of foot length, draw lines perpendicular to the heel and the longest toe, then measure between these two lines.

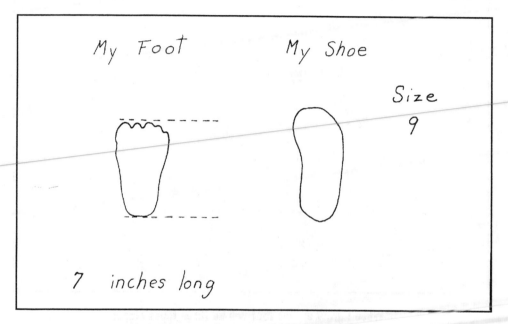

My Foot   My Shoe

Size
9

7 inches long

A tracing of your child's foot and shoe

Hundreds of years ago, before measurements were standardized, units of length were based on the adult human body. For example, a cubit was the distance from the tip of the longest finger on an outstretched hand to the elbow. The measurement we call a foot was the length of the king's foot.

Let your child pretend to be the king or queen and measure the length of the kitchen or lawn. Help your child walk heel to toe, counting each footstep as one "foot." Then count your footsteps and compare the two measurements.

Does your child's birth certificate have his or her footprint? A baby's foot is about one-third the size it will be in adulthood. Your child will enjoy finding the size of, and then drawing, this probable adult footprint by first tracing or drawing three infant-size footprints, one above the other.

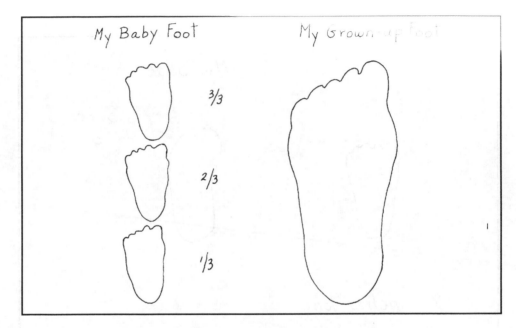

My Baby Foot   My Grown-up Foot

3/3

2/3

1/3

"When I grow up, my foot will be three times bigger than it was when I was born!"

Help your child measure the distance from the wrist to the inside of the elbow. This measurement should correspond to the length of the foot.

The distance from the wrist to the inside of the elbow corresponds to the length of the foot.

Your child will enjoy hearing you read *How Big Is a Foot?* by Rolf Myller. The story explains the need for standard measurements in a lighthearted way.

An interesting fact to share with your child is that although the big toe is larger, it has only two bones while the other toes have three. The foot is very bony—half the bones in the body are contained in the hands and feet.

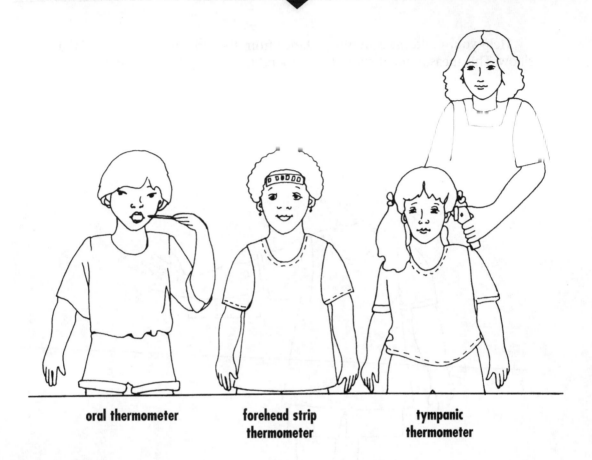

oral thermometer   forehead strip   tympanic
thermometer   thermometer

Temperature

Although many people believe that normal body temperature is 98.6°F (37°C), what is normal for one person is not necessarily normal for another. Many children dislike having their temperatures taken when they are ill and uncomfortable, but it can be an adventure when they are well and have an important question to answer: "What is my normal temperature?"

Take your child's temperature regularly every two or three hours for one day. (This project will be more fun if you have a variety of thermometers to use: oral, forehead strip, and ear or tympanic.) As your child plots each reading on a graph in the record book, the normal fluctuations of temperature will be shown. You may want to vary the activities your child engages in prior to the readings—quiet play or nap time, outdoor play, eating, or relaxing after a bath—to show the effect these activities can have on body temperature.

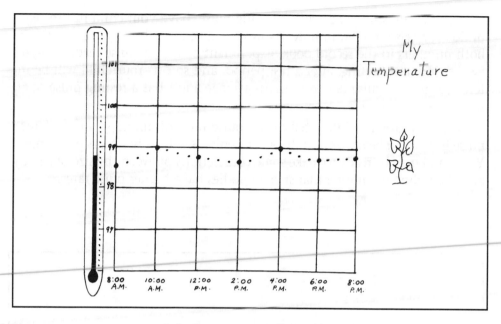

A day's temperature fluctuations

Pulse

Like body temperature, the pulse rate varies according to activity. Record these variations on a page in the record book. This is a good activity to do when your child has a lot of excess energy. Help your child find a pulse point that is easy to feel. Some children may be able to use their middle two fingers to find the wrist pulse, but often the pulse point at the side of the neck—right under the jaw—is easier to find. A six-year-old's resting pulse should be about 90 to 100 beats per minute. For easier counting, split the minute into a 15- or 30-second count.

Two ways to take a pulse

After establishing your child's resting pulse, have your child run in place or do exercises for a few minutes. Now take another pulse reading and record both numbers in the record book. Experiment by taking pulse readings upon awakening, after eating, after a rest period, and so on. Your child will be interested in your pulse rate as well. An average adult has a resting pulse of 60 to 80 beats per minute.

Children are also interested in the pulse rates of animals. An elephant's pulse is 25 to 50 beats per minute. A cat's pulse is 120 to 140 beats per minute. Your child may be ready to make some connections between the size of a body and the pulse rate, noting that smaller bodies have higher pulse rates.

Resting pulse   92

Pulse after   _____
exercise

Record your child's pulse rates.

TEETH

MY LOOSE TOOTH

I had a loose tooth, a wiggly, jiggly loose tooth.
I had a loose tooth, hanging by a thread.
So I pulled my loose tooth, this wiggly jiggly loose tooth,
Put it 'neath the pillow and then I went to bed.
Someone took my loose tooth, my wiggly, jiggly loose tooth.
Now I have a nickel and a hole in my head.

— Anonymous

Has the Tooth Fairy been to your house recently? Children are fascinated by the prospect of losing teeth. Copy or trace the simple tooth diagrams shown

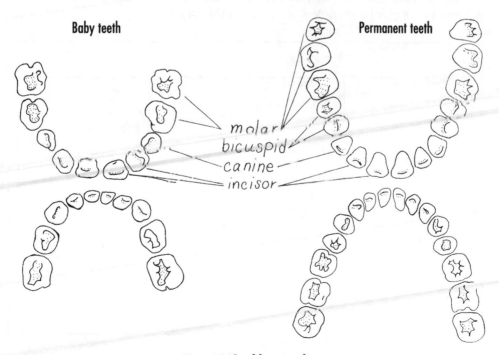

Keep track of lost teeth.

here and add them to the scrapbook. Your child can circle or color in the teeth that have grown in and cross out the ones that have fallen out. Keeping track of teeth is good counting practice. There are 20 baby teeth and 32 permanent teeth. Your child can have fun using a mirror to look into the mouth to count teeth. To see the back teeth, use a small dental mirror, which may be readily purchased.

Your child will be interested to learn that a baby's teeth start growing six months before birth, although they don't make an appearance until much later.

Discuss tooth shape and size with your child. How are "biting" teeth different from "chewing" teeth? Call attention to the long, sharp edges on the biting teeth—the incisors and canines. Then compare these to the rounded, bumpy surfaces of the chewing and grinding teeth—the bicuspids and molars.

You may want to include photos or drawings of your child as an infant with no teeth and of the first tooth and a drawing of the Tooth Fairy. If the Tooth Fairy was kind enough to return your child's first teeth, you might want to tape a Ziploc bag in the scrapbook to contain these treasures. You could then compare the size and shape of your child's baby teeth to the new permanent teeth.

You can also ask your dentist to allow you to take home your child's mouth X rays. These can be included on record book pages as well.

Tooth memories and drawings

A Picture of Me

Children enjoy seeing all of their personal physical statistics on one page of their record book for each stage of growth. You may want to include a photograph or self-portrait of your child. This annual or semi-annual project could be done on a birthday or other special day.

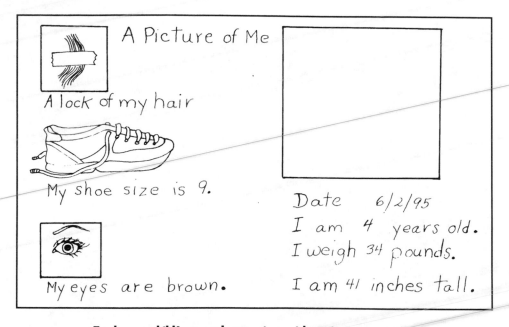

A Picture of Me

A lock of my hair

My shoe size is 9.

My eyes are brown.

Date 6/2/95
I am 4 years old.
I weigh 34 pounds.
I am 41 inches tall.

Track your child's growth over time with anniversary pages.

Chapter 3

Calendar Math

The concept of time is difficult for children to comprehend. Just as children on a lengthy car trip ask, "Are we there yet?" seemingly every five minutes, they may also repeatedly ask their parents, "Is it almost my birthday?" every few weeks.

A calendar is a wonderful tool for teaching children that there is an orderly way to mark the passage of time. Each year we progress through a cycle of days, weeks, and months as seasons change and celestial events occur in the sky. Birthdays and holidays come year after year. It is reassuring to a child to learn that this sequence repeats over and over again and that nature provides clues to help us keep track of time. We can see changes in plants and animals, feel weather changes, and look to the sky for reminders that time passes.

The calendar is rich with opportunities to instill mathematical ideas associated with the measurement of time; for example, sequencing, discovering patterns, counting, estimating, and predicting. Go on a shopping trip with your child to purchase a calendar. Try to find one that has not only pictures that appeal to your child but also large squares to write or draw on. You can begin by noting the days that are special to your family. Go through the calendar and mark family birthdays, planned trips, and holidays. As plans are made and events happen, you can mark play dates with your child's friends, the dates teeth are lost, and the dates of visits from relatives—the possibilities are endless.

This chapter offers suggestions for acquainting your child with the special events that happen monthly in our lives. Feel free to add events that aren't covered here. You will also find suggestions for other math activities that can be used in any month. So the next time your child asks, "Is it almost my birthday?" you can turn to the calendar and explain how to count the days.

JANUARY

MONTHS OF THE YEAR

Thirty days hath September

April, June, and November

All the rest have thirty-one

Except for February alone

And that has twenty-eight days clear

And twenty-nine in each leap year.

Feb.   April
Jan.   March   May   June   July

How Many Days in a Month?

One way for your child to remember how many days are in each month is to learn the poem as you read it aloud. Another way is for children to use the knuckles on their hands.

Close your hand and make a fist. You will see that the knuckles stick up and there are hollows in between.

Start with January on an outside knuckle, going from knuckle to hollow. The months with 31 days land on knuckles. The months with 30 days (or 28 for February) land in the hollows. After tapping for July, start again with August on the knuckle you began with for January.

Sept.   Nov.
Aug.   Oct.   Dec.

Use your knuckles to count the days.

FEBRUARY

MY SHADOW

I have a little shadow that goes in and out with me,

And what can be the use of him is more than I can see.

He is very, very like me from the heels up to the head;

And I see him jump before me, when I jump into my bed.

The funniest thing about him is the way he likes to grow—

Not at all like proper children, which is always very slow;

For he sometimes shoots up taller like an india-rubber ball,

And he sometimes gets so little that there's none of him at all.

He hasn't got a notion of how children ought to play,

And can only make a fool of me in every sort of way.

He stays so close beside me, he's a coward you can see;

I'd think shame to stick to nursie as that shadow sticks to me!

One morning, very early, before the sun was up,

I rose and found the shining dew on every buttercup;

But my lazy little shadow, like an arrant sleepy-head,

Had stayed at home behind me and was fast asleep in bed.

—Robert Louis Stevenson

Groundhog Day

According to an old American folk legend, you can tell how much longer winter will last by watching a groundhog (also called a woodchuck) on February 2. If the ground-hog sees its shadow when it sticks its head out of its burrow, there will be six more weeks of winter weather and the groundhog will go back to sleep. If it doesn't see its shadow, winter's almost over. Spring doesn't officially arrive until March 21, but children love the idea that an animal can forecast the weather. The most famous groundhog is Punxsutawney Phil, who lives in Punxsutawney, Pennsylvania.

Does the groundhog see its shadow on February 2?

You will probably hear news reports about Punxsutawney Phil's outing on Groundhog Day. What would he predict if he lived in your hometown? Go outside on Groundhog Day and see if you and your child cast shadows. Mark the answer in the square for February 2. You can then check back in a couple of months to see whether Phil was correct.

Investigate shadows.

Shadows are fun to investigate. This is something that can be done on walks throughout the year, not just on Groundhog Day. As your child learns to notice shadows, you can call attention to the way they grow longer or shorter at different times of day and from season to season as the sun shifts position in the sky. Are shadows longer or shorter in the morning, at noon, or in the evening? In summer or in winter?

Leap Year

It takes the earth about 365 days and 6 hours to make one orbit around the sun. We call 365 days a year. But what about the extra 6 hours? In 4 years, those extra hours add up to one whole day. We put this day at the end of February—February 29—every 4 years. A year that includes a twenty-ninth day in February is called a leap year and has 366 days.

Explore the idea that a child born on February 29 would have a "real" birthday only every 4 years. Most people born on February 29 (leap day) celebrate their birthday on February 28.

Help your child calculate how many years it would take a "leap-year baby" to reach your child's age if the birthday is celebrated only on February 29.

4 years to reach age 1

8 years to reach age 2

12 years to reach age 3

16 years to reach age 4

20 years to reach age 5

24 years to reach age 6

MARCH

A SONG FOR MARCH

Who has seen the wind?
Neither I nor you.
But when the leaves hang trembling,
The wind is passing through.
Who has seen the wind?
Neither you nor I:
But when the trees bow down their heads,
The wind is passing by.

—Christina Rossetti

In like a lion...

...out like a lamb.

In many parts of the country, March is the windiest month of the year. There is a saying, "March comes in like a lion and goes out like a lamb." Help your child draw a lion in the square for March 1, and a lamb in the square for March 31. Discuss the types of weather that could be associated with lions or lambs. For example, does the wind seem to roar like a lion? When the wind stops, are the soft breezes gentle as a lamb? Put lions in the squares on days with lionlike weather, and lambs on days with lamblike weather. Add them up at the end of the month and see which kind of weather occurred more often. Is there a pattern? Did the saying prove true this year?

◆◆◆

FOUR SEASONS

Spring is showery, flowery, bowery.
Summer: hoppy, choppy, poppy.
Autumn: wheezy, sneezy, freezy.
Winter: slippy, drippy, nippy.

—Anonymous

◆◆◆

The words in this poem are commonly associated with the seasons. They may or may not be true of the weather in your part of the country. The typical symbols of fall—orange and red falling leaves—may be confusing to your child if leaves on the trees in your hometown don't turn colors and fall off the trees. Similarly, snow is difficult to imagine when one has never played in it.

The weather page in your newspaper is rich with data, much of which is organized as charts and graphs. Most weather pages also have maps that display symbols to indicate weather conditions and numbers to indicate temperatures. Some weather maps are printed in color to make temperature comparisons easier. Most weather pages print the times of sunrise and sunset, and many display symbols to show the current phase of the moon.

With some guidance, children can locate their hometown on these maps and interpret the weather information that they find. They can certainly read temperatures and learn the symbols for sun, rain, clouds, and snow. Look at the page with your child and note the weather in your area. Then look at the weather in other parts of the country, perhaps where relatives and friends live. Discuss the differences or similarities. Find the warmest place in the country; the coldest. These activities are opportunities for your child to begin to locate and interpret data.

The Vernal Equinox

Depending on the year, March 20 or March 21 is the spring, or vernal, equinox in the Northern Hemisphere. This is one of two days in the year when the hours of daytime and nighttime are equal, or the same: 12. It is the first day of spring. Find out when the vernal equinox occurs this year. Put an equal sign (=) on the square for this day. Explore the concept of equal by playing with balance scales, pouring equal amounts of water into containers, or serving equal portions of a favorite food to family members.

This month, help your child note the time of sunset, or the beginning of nighttime, each day. Keep a record of the time of sunset on the calendar. Point out that the time of sunset changes as the days get longer.

APRIL AND MAY

Blackbird, whistle,

Woodpecker, drum,

Spring has come, spring has come.

Cardinal, sing in the apple tree,

Spring is here for you and me.

Longer days, shorter nights,

Boys and girls, bring out your kites.

—Anonymous

Daylight Saving Time

In most parts of the United States, the first Sunday in April means the beginning of daylight saving time. On this day, the clocks are set ahead 1 hour. This is usually done at bedtime the night before. That way we don't have to wake up at 2 o'clock in the morning, when daylight saving time officially begins. We have daylight saving time so that it is light an hour longer in the evening when most of us are awake, rather than in the very early morning when many of us are still asleep.

Wondering about 100

The hundredth day of the year occurs in April. With your child, start on January 1 and, on the calendar, count each day until you get to 100. Write 100 in that square. Counting to 100 is a real accomplishment for a child. Reinforce this skill by helping your child make a special collection of 100 items. Some suggestions of things to save are buttons, pennies, sports cards or other collectible cards, marbles, bottle caps or pull tabs, stamps, beans, paper clips, and postcards.

The Growing Season

RAIN

The rain is raining all around,
It falls on field and tree
It rains on the umbrellas here,
And on the ships at sea.

—Robert Louis Stevenson

In many parts of the country, it rains a lot in April and May. Your child can keep track of rainy days by drawing raindrops in the square of the dates it rains in April and May. Then count the rainy days in each month, compare the totals, and ask, "Does it rain more in April or in May?"

There is but one May in the year,
And sometimes May is wet and cold:
There is but one May in the year
Before the year grows old.

Yet though it be the chilliest May,
With least of sun and most of showers,
Its wind and dew, its night and day,
Bring up the flowers.

—Christina Rossetti

"April showers bring May flowers," as the saying goes. These may be the perfect months to try the planting and seed growing experiences described in chapter 1. Use the calendar to keep track of when the seeds are planted, when the first shoots of green appear, and how tall the plants get as they grow.

Arbor Day is still celebrated in April or May in many communities in the United States. It is a time to plant new trees and admire old ones. Earth Day is celebrated on April 22. This is a day set aside to make people aware of ways to keep our planet healthy.

JUNE

OUR FLAG

Hail to the thirteen
Bright, bright bars;
Hail to the fifty
White, white stars.
Freely and brightly they float in the breeze,
On mountain peaks, and plains, and seas.

Hail to our flag—
Red, white, and blue.
Long may our colors,
When placed in view,
Tell of a nation proud to be
"The home of the brave" and "the land of the free."

—Anonymous

The first U.S. flag

Flag Fun

June 14 is Flag Day in the United States. On this day in 1777, the design that has been the basis of all subsequent American flags was adopted. Tell your child the story of Betsy Ross: Betsy Ross was a seamstress who worked in Philadelphia in the 1700s. It is said that she was asked by General George Washington to make a flag using his design of 13 stripes and a circle of 13 stars. The stars and stripes represented the 13 colonies in the country at that time. Betsy Ross's flag became the first official American flag in 1777.

The current U.S. flag

The U.S. flag provides many opportunities to enrich mathematical understandings of patterns and counting. Help your child count the stars on the flag. Point out that a star is added each time a new state is made part of our country. The last two stars—the forty-ninth and fiftieth—were added for Alaska and Hawaii, respectively. The stars are arranged into patterns, which makes them easier to count. There are

5 rows of 6 stars (5 × 6 = <u>30 stars</u>)

and

4 rows of 5 stars (4 × 5 = <u>20 stars</u>)

to make <u>50 stars</u> in all.

Although the number of stars has changed over the years, the 13 stripes have remained the same, representing the original 13 colonies. Help your child see that stripes are rectangles. The stripes alternate red and white, starting with red. Since 13 is an odd number, there is one more red stripe than there are white stripes.

Your child may color a red, white, and blue pattern on the June calendar page squares. Another enjoyable way to learn more about pattern and shape is to create a new flag. Stars, stripes, and the field of blue can be used to make a different design. For example, the field of blue could be placed in the middle of the flag with vertical stripes surrounding it.

It is interesting to note that many other countries use the same colors and shapes as the U.S. flag but in different arrangements. For example, the flags of the United Kingdom, Norway, and New Zealand are each red, white, and blue and use stripes in their designs. Can you find more? Look in a book of flags or the flag section of an encyclopedia.

Children may want to design their own personal or family flag. Use any combination of color, pattern, and shape to make a unique and pleasing flag.

Summer Solstice

BED IN SUMMER

In winter I get up at night
And dress by yellow candle-light.
In summer quite the other way,
I have to go to bed by day.

I have to go to bed and see
The birds still hopping on the tree,
Or hear the grown-up people's feet
Still going past me in the street.

And does it not seem hard to you,
When all the sky is clear and blue,
And I should like so much to play,
To have to go to bed by day?

—Robert Louis Stevenson

The summer solstice occurs around June 21. It is the first day of summer in the Northern Hemisphere. It is the longest day of the year from sunrise to sunset. The sun is at its highest position of the year at noon.

Celebrate the beginning of summer and the longest day of the year with an especially long picnic.

Enjoy lo-o-o-o-ng foods such as:

- foot-long hot dogs
- submarine sandwiches
- spaghetti
- corn on the cob
- string beans
- breadsticks

- dill pickles
- cucumbers—cut lengthwise
- carrots—cut lengthwise
- licorice sticks
- banana splits

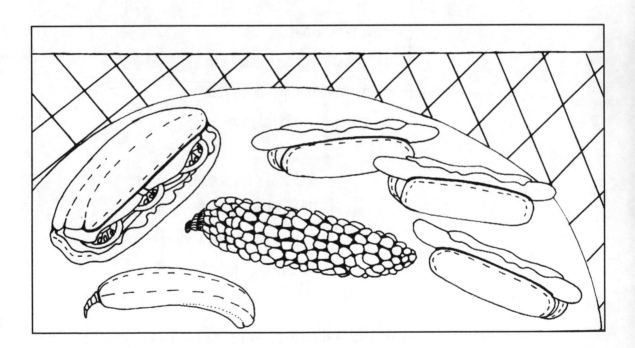

Enjoy a lo-o-o-o-ong picnic.

JULY

◆◆◆ TO JULY ◆◆◆

Here's to July,

Here's to July,

For the bird,

And the bee,

And the butterfly;

For the flowers

That blossom

For feasting the eye;

For skates, ball,

And jump ropes,

For swings that go high;

For rockety

Fireworks that

Blaze in the sky,

Oh, here's to July.

—Anonymous

The Fourth of July

July 4 is the birthday of the United States, which was founded on that date in 1776. Your child can draw a birthday candle in the July 4 square. This is a good time to talk about birthdays. How old is our country? How big would a birthday cake have to be to fit that many candles? Make sure that all family birthdays are marked on the calendar.

AUGUST

AUGUST HEAT

In August, when the days are hot,
I like to find a shady spot,
And hardly move a single bit—
And sit—
And sit—
And sit—
And sit.

—Anonymous

The Dog Days of Summer

August often has the very hottest days of the summer. These are referred to as the dog days of summer because Sirius, the Dog Star, can be seen close to sunrise at this time of year. Sirius is called the Dog Star because it is part of the constellation Canis Major, the Great Dog. It is the brightest star in the sky. Buy an outdoor thermometer for your home and help your child learn to read it. Children unfamiliar with reading scales, such as a thermometer, can learn more easily by associating temperature with color.

Buy the largest thermometer available and color code it with markers or colored tape. The breakdown shown here works well.

Children can practice reading the number that aligns with the top of the fluid in the thermometer. They will begin to associate the higher numbers, at the top of the thermometer, with warm and hot

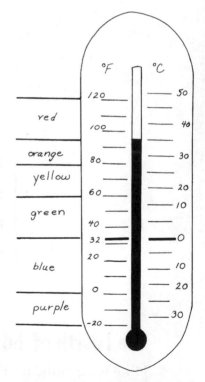

Thermometers can be color-coded to help children associate color with temperature.

weather and with orange and red colors. The more moderate temperatures fall into the yellow range, and the colder temperatures are represented by blue and purple—at the bottom of the thermometer.

Record the temperature on as many days in August as possible. Your child can write the temperature in each calendar square and color the square to correspond to the temperature. At the end of the month, you can help your child find and circle the date with the hottest temperature.

This would be a good time to practice using the other types of body thermometers—oral, forehead strip, and ear (tympanic)—and other thermometers commonly found around the house, such as oven and meat thermometers. Discuss what hot means with your child. For instance, explain the difference between a hot oven—400°F (200°C)—and a hot day—100°F (38°C). What temperature is hot when your child has a fever? What temperature is "done" for a piece of meat? You can find a table of meat cooking temperatures in most cookbooks. Talk about why it is refreshing to have an iced drink on a hot August day, and explain that water freezes at 32°F (0°C).

SEPTEMBER

The Autumnal Equinox

Even though the days are pretty long and winter seems far away, each day has been getting a little shorter since the summer solstice, the longest day. Now, on September 22 or 23—the fall, or autumnal, equinox—the hours of daytime and nighttime are equal again. After this date, the nights will be longer than the days.

Your child can divide the square for the autumnal equinox in half. Color one half yellow to represent the day and the other half black to represent the night.

Moon Musings

OLD MAN MOON

The moon is very, very old.
The reason why is clear—
he gets his birthday once a month,
instead of once a year.

—Aileen Fisher

COMMA IN THE SKY

A comma hung above the park,
a shiny punctuation mark;
we saw it curving in the dark
the night the moon was new.

A period hung above the bay,
immense though it was far away;
we saw it at the end of day
the night the moon was full.

—Aileen Fisher

For centuries, people have kept track of time by watching the phases of the moon. Children are captivated by the image of the Man in the Moon. Look at the moon together each night that it is visible and discuss its phases. Most newspaper weather pages include information about phases of the moon, moonrise, and moonset.

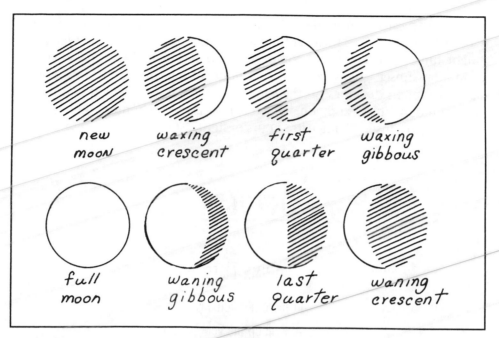

new
moon

waxing
crescent

first
quarter

waxing
gibbous

full
moon

waning
gibbous

last
quarter

waning
crescent

Phases of the moon

As you and your child observe the moon, you can reinforce several important concepts. Here are some suggestions:

SIZE COMPARISONS	"Is tonight's moon bigger or smaller than last night's?" "How big do you think tomorrow's moon will be?"
SHAPE	"What is the shape of a full moon?" "The quarter moon looks like a semi-circle, doesn't it?"
MOON COOKIES	Bake large sugar cookies with your child. Shape them into phases of the moon by cutting circles, semicircles, and crescents.

The expression "once in a blue moon" describes something that almost never happens. Blue moon is the name given to the second full moon in a single month's time. It is a rare occurrence but one that is worth looking for and one that will intrigue children. Perhaps special wishes can be wished on this moon.

The harvest moon is the full moon during the harvest season—the one closest to September 23, the autumnal equinox. It is often a very large and bright full moon. The name comes from the fact that this moon rises very soon after sunset, giving farmers extra hours of light for the harvest season. Put large moon drawings on the squares of the dates on which you see the harvest moon. The next moon, in October, is called the hunter's moon. It also rises close to sunset, giving extra hours of light.

OCTOBER

AUTUMN FIRES

In the other gardens
And all up the vale,
From the autumn bonfires
See the smoke trail!

Pleasant summer over
And all the summer flowers.
The red fire blazes,
The gray smoke towers.

Sing a song of seasons!
Something's bright in all!
Flowers in the summer,
Fires in the fall!

—Robert Louis Stevenson

Standard Time

On the last Sunday in October, daylight saving time ends and we go back to standard time. Teach your child the phrase "spring forward, fall back." This reminds us which way the clock is turned the night before. Talk about forward and back and what these concepts mean. Perhaps you could give your child an old clock to play with. Children can learn to set the hour forward or back even though the concept of telling time may be too advanced right now.

Fall Colors

In many areas of the country, the leaves are still green at the beginning of October. But by this time in other parts of the country, they have begun to turn colors, and by the end of October the leaves are falling. Help your child cut out leaves made of orange, yellow, and red paper. These can be pasted on the calendar to designate the days when leaves are falling in your part of the country.

Halloween

Our present holiday customs of dressing in costume and carving pumpkins originated with the ancient Druid people in Europe. The holiday was a harvest festival, celebrating the bounty of the fields and marking the winter animal-breeding season. Vegetables were hollowed out to accommodate candles, and people danced in the field. Later, the holiday became All Hallows' Eve, a time to honor saints. People dressed as ghosts and witches to frighten off evil spirits.

Your child may wish to paste a paper jack-o'-lantern on the calendar square for Halloween.

November

The North Wind Doth Blow

The north wind doth blow,
And we shall have snow,
And what will the robin do then, poor thing?
He'll sit in a barn,
And keep himself warm,
And hide his head under his wing, poor thing!

The north wind doth blow,
And we shall have snow,
And what will the swallow do then, poor thing?
Oh, do you not know
That he's off long ago,
To a country where he will find spring, poor thing!

The north wind doth blow,
And we shall have snow,
And what will the dormouse do then, poor thing?
Roll'd up like a ball,
In his nest snug and small,
He'll sleep till warm weather comes in, poor thing!

The north wind doth blow,
And we shall have snow,
And what will the honey-bee do then, poor thing?
In his hive he will stay
Till the cold is away,
And then he'll come out in the spring, poor thing!

The north wind doth blow,
And we shall have snow,
And what will the children do then, poor things?
When lessons are done,
They must skip, jump and run,
Until they have made themselves warm, poor things!

—Anonymous

If you live in a northern climate, the month of November usually brings the first very cold, windy days and the snows of late fall. Those who live in southern climates will not experience such dramatic changes, but children can be encouraged to notice seasonal differences in temperature, weather, vegetation, and animal population.

As the poem notes, animals handle weather changes in different ways. Humans put on more layers of warm clothing, turn up the thermostat, and "skip, jump and run" to make themselves warm. Other animals spend more time inside barns, zoo enclosures, and homes to keep themselves warm. Your child may notice that the fur of family pets grows thicker during cold weather. Some animals, especially birds, migrate to warmer climates as winter approaches, and you may notice formations of birds flying south. Some animals, such as the dormouse mentioned in the poem, hibernate in winter. When animals hibernate, they enter long periods of deep sleep or inactivity. Other hibernating animals include bears, chipmunks, bats, reptiles, and some insects, such as the honey-bee in the poem.

This is a wonderful time of the year to sharpen senses of observation. As your child sees signs of the impending winter, notes can be made on the calendar. Perhaps a flock of birds can be drawn in the square to mark the dates when migrating birds are seen in the sky. How many are in the flock? A trip to the zoo at this time of year can offer children glimpses of hibernating animals. You may also wish to do some of the outdoor temperature–measuring activities described for August.

Look for opportunities to engage your child in counting, measuring, and predicting activities. Could the density of the family dog's fur be noted in fall and then again in spring? Can animal footprints be spotted in the snow? What might this animal be, and how does it survive the winter? At what temperature is a sweater or jacket needed for outdoor play?

Thanksgiving

Thanksgiving is always the fourth Thursday of November in the United States and the second Tuesday of October in Canada. Have your child count the number of Thursdays in November this year. On what date is Thanksgiving?

If you are planning a family feast, this is a good time for your child to get some cooking experience. See "Cooking" in chapter 1 for some ideas on how to include children in cooking chores.

December

Falling Snow

See the pretty snowflakes
Falling from the sky;
On the walk and housetop
Soft and thick they lie.

On the window-ledges
On the branches bare;
Now how fast they gather,
Filling all the air.

Look into the garden,
Where the grass was green;
Covered by the snowflakes,
Not a blade is seen.

Now the bare black bushes
All look soft and white,
Every twig is laden—
What a pretty sight.

—Anonymous

Winter Solstice

The winter solstice occurs around December 21. This is the first day of winter in the Northern Hemisphere. It is the shortest day of the year—just the opposite of the summer solstice in June, the longest day. At noon on the winter solstice, the sun is at its lowest noon position in the sky. Your child can circle this date on the calendar.

Counting the Days of Holidays

Many families celebrate holidays in December. These holidays often involve counting days in some way, such as opening the 25 windows of an Advent calendar one day at a time, counting and singing about the 12 days of Christmas, and lighting candles for each of the 8 days of Hanukkah and the seven days of Kwanzaa. If your family celebrates any of these holidays, mark the days on the calendar.

New Year's Eve

December 31 marks the end of the old year and the beginning of the new year. This is an important time for children to learn about cycles—one thing ends and another begins, repeating over and over again. Talk about New Year's resolutions, and help your child draw up a short list of things to do or change in the new year. Explain that the symbols of New Year's Eve are an old man (Father Time) who represents the old year, and a baby, who represents the new year. These symbols commonly appear in newspapers and magazines and on television at this time of year.

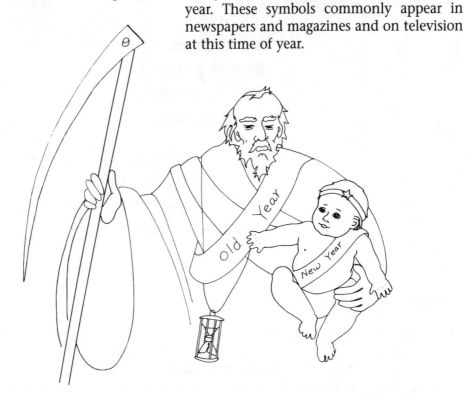

Up the Hill, Down the Hill

Old One, lie down,
Your journey is done,
Little New Year
Will rise with the sun.
Now you have come to
The foot of the hill,
Lay down your bones,
Old Year, and lie still.

Young One, step out,
Your journey's begun,
Weary Old Year
Makes way for his son.
Now you have started
To climb up the hill,
Put best foot forward,
New Year, with a will.

Up the hill, down the hill,
Which is the best?
Up-hill is labour,
and down-hill is rest.
—**Anonymous**

MONTHLY MATH ACTIVITIES

A calendar is filled, because of its repetitive nature, with possibilities for teaching children about numbers and patterns. Repetition not only provides children with enjoyment, but also reinforces important concepts. Your child may want to count all the way to 30 (or 31) each month or alternate with practice counting backward. Do as much or as little as your child desires. Following are some suggestions of counting activities to use with your child on the calendar.

Each month, your child can use the "Months of the Year" poem or the knuckle method to tell how many days are in the month. You can discuss how

Calendar Counting

January						
Sunday	Monday	Tuesday	Wednesday	Thursday	Friday	Saturday
						①
②	③	④	⑤	⑥	⑦	⑧
⑨	⑩	11	12	13	14	15
16	17	18	19	20	21	22
23 30	24 31	25	26	27	28	29

Circle the numbers from 1 to 10.

February						
Sunday	Monday	Tuesday	Wednesday	Thursday	Friday	Saturday
		1	2	3	4	5
6	7	8	9	10	⑪	⑫
⑬	⑭	⑮	⑯	⑰	⑱	⑲
⑳	21	22	23	24	25	26
27	28	29				

Circle the numbers from 11 to 20.

March						
Sunday	Monday	Tuesday	Wednesday	Thursday	Friday	Saturday
				1	2	3	4
5	6	7	8	9	10	11
12	13	14	15	16	17	18
19	20	㉑	㉒	㉓	㉔	㉕
㉖	㉗	㉘	㉙	㉚	㉛	

Circle the numbers from 21 to 31.

April						
Sunday	Monday	Tuesday	Wednesday	Thursday	Friday	Saturday
						1
②	3	④	5	⑥	7	⑧
9	⑩	11	⑫	13	⑭	15
⑯	17	⑱	19	⑳	21	㉒
23 30	㉔	25	㉖	27	㉘	29

Circle the even numbers.

May

Sunday	Monday	Tuesday	Wednesday	Thursday	Friday	Saturday
	(1)	2	(3)	4	(5)	6
(7)	8	(9)	10	(11)	12	(13)
14	(15)	16	(17)	18	(19)	20
(21)	22	(23)	24	(25)	26	(27)
28	(29)	30	(31)			

Circle the odd numbers.

June

Sunday	Monday	Tuesday	Wednesday	Thursday	Friday	Saturday
				(1)	(2)	(3)
(4)	(5)	(6)	(7)	(8)	(9)	(10)
(11)	(12)	(13)	(14)	(15)	(16)	(17)
(18)	(19)	(20)	(21)	(22)	(23)	(24)
(25)	(26)	(27)	(28)	(29)	(30)	

Circle the numbers from 1 to 30.

July

Sunday	Monday	Tuesday	Wednesday	Thursday	Friday	Saturday
						(1)
(2)	(3)	(4)	(5)	(6)	(7)	(8)
(9)	(10)	11	12	13	14	15
16	17	18	19	20	21	22
23 / 30	24 / 31	25	26	27	28	29

Count backward from 10.

August

Sunday	Monday	Tuesday	Wednesday	Thursday	Friday	Saturday
		1	2	3	4	(5)
6	7	8	9	(10)	11	12
13	14	(15)	16	17	18	19
(20)	21	22	23	24	25	26
27	28	29	(30)	31		

Count by fives.

September

Sunday	Monday	Tuesday	Wednesday	Thursday	Friday	Saturday
					1	2
3	4	5	6	7	8	9
(10)	11	12	13	14	15	16
17	18	19	(20)	21	22	23
24	25	26	27	28	29	(30)

Count by tens.

many weeks are in the month. How many are full weeks? If the month begins or ends in the middle of a week, how many days are "missing" that week?

Wonderful poems about the months, seasons, holidays, and weather can be found in most children's poetry anthologies. You will enjoy reading these aloud together. Your child may even commit some of the shorter ones to memory as you read them again and again.

CALENDAR PATTERNS

The calendar is a natural place to make patterns. The drawings that follow illustrate a variety of patterns that can be drawn on a calendar. Children may also want to create their own patterns. These patterns could be repeating sequences of two, three, or more shapes, designs or colors.

Creating Calendar Patterns

January

Sunday	Monday	Tuesday	Wednesday	Thursday	Friday	Saturday
						1
2	3	4	5	6	7	8
9	10	11	12	13	14	15
16	17	18	19	20	21	22
23	24	25	26	27	28	29
30	31					

Color the diagonals.

February

Sunday	Monday	Tuesday	Wednesday	Thursday	Friday	Saturday
		1	2	3	4	5
6	7	8	9	10	11	12
13	14	15	16	17	18	19
20	21	22	23	24	25	26
27	28	29				

Color the odd-numbered squares.

March

Sunday	Monday	Tuesday	Wednesday	Thursday	Friday	Saturday
				1	2	3
4	5	6	7	8	9	10
11	12	13	14	15	16	17
18	19	20	21	22	23	24
25	26	27	28	29	30	31

Color the even-numbered squares.

April

Sunday	Monday	Tuesday	Wednesday	Thursday	Friday	Saturday
1	2	3	4	5	6	7
8	9	10	11	12	13	14
15	16	17	18	19	20	21
22	23	24	25	26	27	28
29	30					

Color the first and last days of the week.

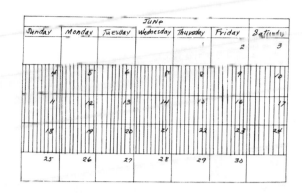

May

Sunday	Monday	Tuesday	Wednesday	Thursday	Friday	Saturday
		1	2	3	4	5	6

(See calendar image)

Color the week with the fewest days.

Color the weeks with 7 days.

Try these or create your own.

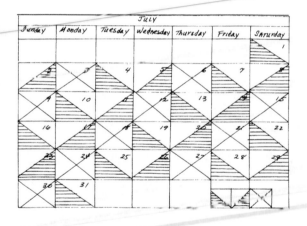

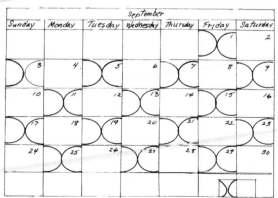

Chapter 4

Math on the Move

N ow it is time for you and your child to move out of the house, into the neighborhood and beyond, in your search for mathematical experiences. Don't feel under pressure to make up questions for your child or elicit responses. Sharing sights, insights, and experiences in a relaxed, casual way will bring you closer to your goal of broadening your child's mathematical horizons.

ON FOOT

Street Address Numbers

Figuring out our street address system is an interesting mathematical task. Begin by pointing out the address number of your house or apartment building. As you walk up or down the street, what happens to the numbers on the various buildings? Do the numbers on the opposite side of the street differ from the ones on your side in any consistent manner? (This assumes an ability to differentiate between odd and even numbers.) Is there a relationship between the numbered streets and the house numbers? Remember not to try to put together all the pieces of this puzzle on one walk.

Fences

Keep a record of the fences you pass on your walk. How many do you pass? From what materials are they made? How many are wooden, wire, iron, brick, stone, cement, or hedge? How many different styles within these categories? Depending on where you walk, you might see the following kinds of wooden fences: board, stockade, picket or pale, lattice or trellis, rail, dike or others. Counting and categorizing are valuable math tools.

Some basic math terms you can use to describe the fences you see on your walk are

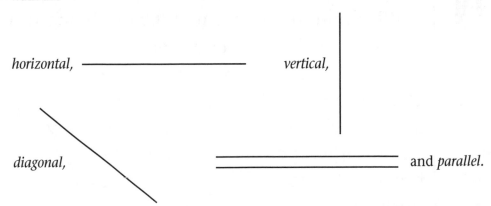

horizontal, ———————— *vertical,*

diagonal, ———————— and *parallel.*

Some positional terms to use

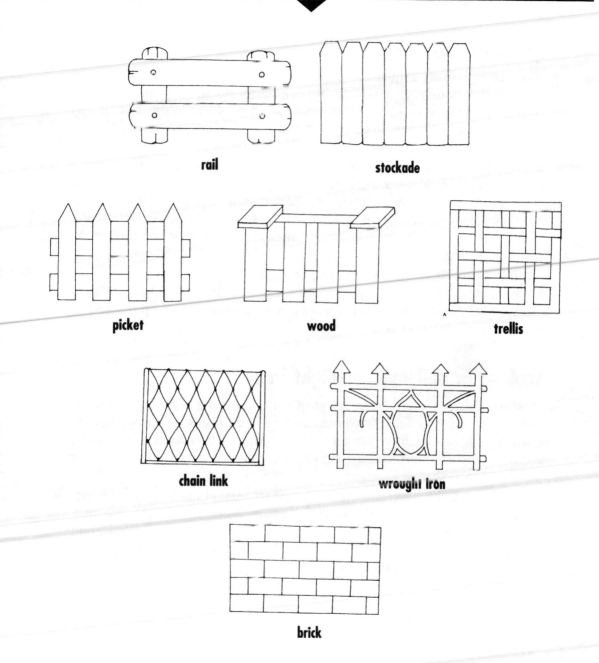

rail

stockade

picket

wood

trellis

chain link

wrought iron

brick

Different kinds of fences

Measuring Distances

A city block is often a square, so walking around the block is walking around a square. The term block also stands for one side of the square, from corner to corner. In some areas there is a standard number of blocks to the mile. If this is true in your area, help your child figure out whether you have walked a mile, or two miles, or one-half mile.

Another interesting way children can check the distance they have walked is by wearing a pedometer. These inexpensive little gadgets measure distance by responding to the wearer's body motion at each step. In order to have it run accurately, one must measure and record the length of the wearer's stride. This is a good excuse to get out the tape measure and help young walkers do some measuring.

To measure stride, put a mark at your child's toe. Ask your child to take a natural walking step, and put another mark at the forward heel. Then, measure the distance between the marks, being careful to line up the end of the tape measure with the first mark.

Looking at Buildings: Straight Lines

Many city buildings have been designed with an emphasis on straight lines. You and your young walking companion might first seek out these. Besides being a study of straight versus curved lines, you can also use this walk as an excellent opportunity to begin familiarizing your child with the names of plane and solid shapes.

Here are some basic geometric terms that are useful in talking about buildings: *straight line* and *curved line*, *circle*, *square*, *rectangle*, *triangle*, *trapezoid*, *rhombus (diamond)*, *cube*, *rectangular prism*, *sphere*, *cylinder*, *cone*, *pyramid*, and *hemisphere*. Children often enjoy experimenting with this terminology if you don't overwhelm them with it all at once.

As you walk, you might see some of these building designs:

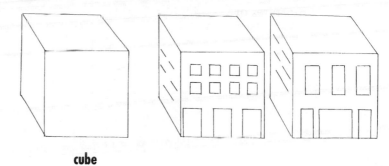

- neat cubes with rectangular doors and windows, arranged in even arrays

cube

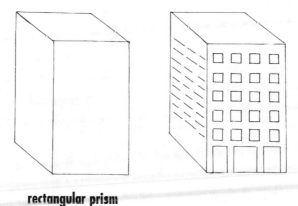

- tall and lean rectangular prisms

rectangular prism

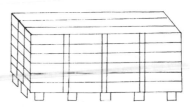

- short and wide rectangular prisms

rectangular prism

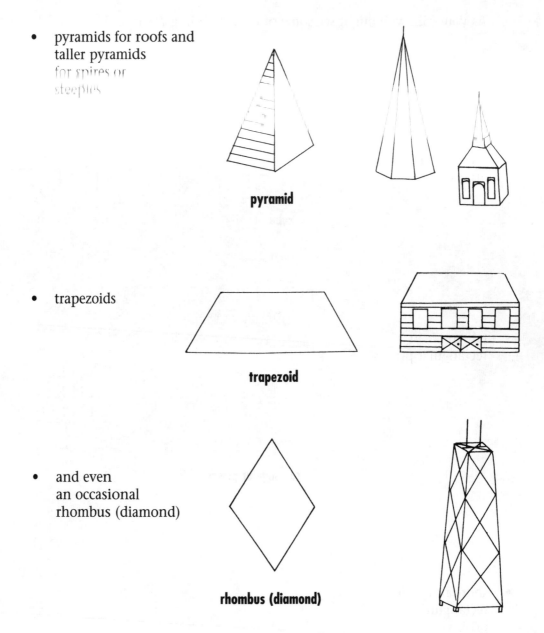

- pyramids for roofs and taller pyramids for spires or steeples

pyramid

- trapezoids

trapezoid

- and even an occasional rhombus (diamond)

rhombus (diamond)

Young city hikers should be able to find a wide variety of plane and three-dimensional shapes as they study architectural facades.

Looking at Buildings: Curved Lines

Children may also want to look for curved lines in the walls, arches, and windows of buildings as they continue on their architectural walk.

They may find a variety of cylindrical buildings,

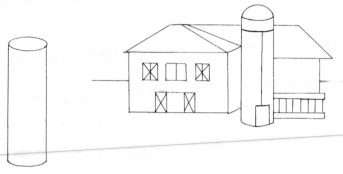

cylinder

or buildings with a combination of curved and straight lines.

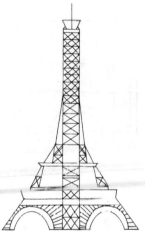

They may find roofs that are cones or hemispheres (domes),

  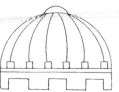

cone

hemisphere

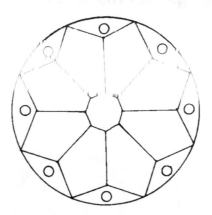

beautiful circular windows,

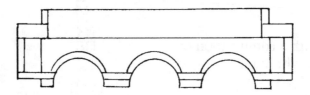

and a variety of arches.

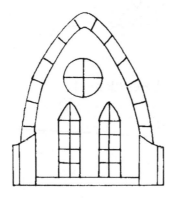

AT THE PLAYGROUND

It's hard for children to escape math and physics at the playground, home of the simple machine. If they take a turn on the slide, they are climbing up a ladder and sliding down an inclined plane. If they run off to the swings to soar up into the blue, they are swinging on pendulums, overcoming the forces of inertia and gravity. When they play on the seesaw, they are going up and down, experimenting with a balance beam that rests on a fulcrum or a spring. Then there are horizontal ladders to traverse, hand over hand, and vertical poles to shinny. Sometimes there are parallel bars as well. Finally, if they decide they just want to sit this one out in the sandbox, quietly playing with their pails and shovels, they are still doing math as they experiment with volume.

horizontal ladder

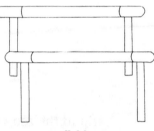

parallel bars

It is not necessary to ask specific questions to create a mathematical awareness in children. In playing on the equipment, they are doing math and physics with their whole bodies. They will learn to verbalize their experiences as they hear you using terms such as *up, down, around, high, higher, low, lower, under, over, across, beginning, end, fast, slow, big, little, horizontal, vertical,* and *parallel.*

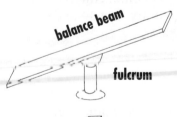

balance beam

fulcrum

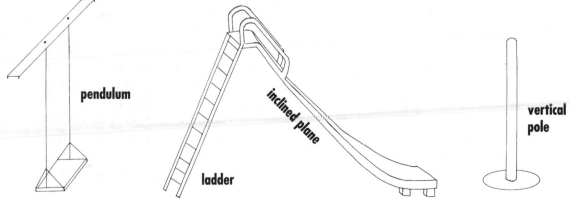

pendulum

ladder

inclined plane

vertical pole

A Trip to the Zoo

Can You Find?

Can you find
An animal with zero tails?
And one with one long nose?
A deer with two long wavy horns?
Or feet with just three toes?
Four legs should not be hard to find.
But five nonhuman fingers?
Six-legged creatures won't stay caged.
(Be careful of their stingers.)

—Kate Morrison

A trip to the zoo can be an ideal outing for animal lovers, people watchers, and the math-action minded. While strolling from habitat to habitat, children will naturally be looking for patterns, counting, making comparisons—and perhaps buying some refreshments.

Money Matters

Giving children the opportunity to handle the money for their admission ticket is a valuable experience, even if they are as yet unable to count out the exact change.

You may also want to give your child a set amount to spend on refreshments and then help calculate what the money can buy. Or help your child to count out the money needed for a specific refreshment and to decide whether $1 is too much or too little. Children can get satisfaction and gain confidence by being in charge of small amounts of money if the task is simple enough. Take your cue from your child. If there is interest, you are on the right track. If there is none, take it up at another time.

For a fuller discussion of money, see "At the Grocery Store," later in this chapter.

Zoo Patterns

Searching for patterns can be a fascinating way to look at animals. The markings of some animal species serve as camouflage, helping them blend into their native surroundings. Giraffes, zebras, leopards, and snakes are examples of animals with dramatically patterned markings. There are many others. Children often enjoy trying to capture what they see on paper with pencil, markers, or crayons. Drawing the patterns you find together could give a focus to your pattern treasure hunt and be a nice souvenir as well.

Can you identify these animal patterns? (See answers below.)

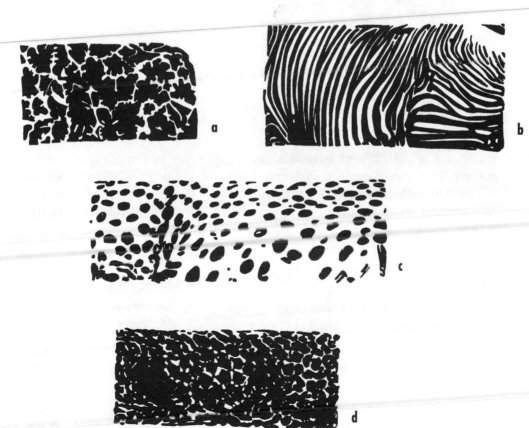

a. giraffe; b. zebra; c. cheetah; d. leopard

IN THE CAR

"Are We Almost There?"

A long car trip can be an endurance test for young passengers and their parents, or it can be an opportunity for an interesting set of challenges. First the focus must shift away from destination fixation to the many interesting games there are to play en route. Begin by trying to figure out how many different ways there are of expressing one's impatience and anticipation:

> "Are we almost there?"
>
> "How soon?"
>
> "How much longer?"
>
> "How much farther?"
>
> "How many more miles?"
>
> "Today?"
>
> "Tomorrow?"
>
> "The day after?"

Counting the different ways of asking the question is a mathematical task in itself. The answer can run well into double-digit numbers, given a persistent and impatient traveler. Even more valuable is the ability to frame and find answers to these questions about distance traveled and the passage of time.

Time

Young children like to use, but often confuse, terms such as *yesterday, today,* and *tomorrow.* Explaining terms as you use them can be a help.

> *Child:*   Are we going to get there yesterday?
>
> *Parent:*   Yesterday was the day we packed our suitcases. We're going to arrive tomorrow afternoon.
>
> *Child:*   When's tomorrow?
>
> *Parent:*   It's not the day we're in now. That's today. Tomorrow is always the day after today. We'll drive all morning, stop for lunch, drive all afternoon, eat dinner, and spend the night at a campsite. We'll get up tomorrow morning—the morning after this morning—have breakfast, drive until lunchtime, eat, drive some more, and arrive between lunch and dinnertime. That will be tomorrow afternoon.

After this recitation, you'll probably all be wishing you could get there yesterday. If young passengers can see the car clock, you can help them be responsible for notifying the driver that a certain amount of time (such as an hour) has passed and it is time to switch drivers or take a break.

Distance

Keeping track of mileage is a good way for children to learn more about our base ten number system. Most highways in the U.S. interstate highway system have mile markers. In many cases, the exit numbers correspond to miles traveled on a particular highway. For example, Exit 21 on the Indiana Tollway is 21 miles from the western border of the state. Exit numbers increase as you travel from west to east and from south to north. Children will see how the numbers change first in the ones place, then in the tens place, then in the hundreds place. Traveling south and west may improve your child's ability to count backward.

Fuel-Tank Fractions

Show the fuel gauge to your child as you discuss the status of the fuel tank. This is a natural way to introduce children to fractions: "Our fuel gauge is on the one-half mark. When it drops to the one–quarter mark, we should begin looking for a gas station." After you have filled up your tank and turned on the ignition, it is fun for children to watch the gauge indicator move from empty to full.

Stopping for Gas

Watching the dollar amounts soar on the gas tank register may be painful for you, but watching the changes in the numbers of both gallons and dollars is a good exercise for your young mathematician. As always, being in on the actual purchase is a good experience.

Road Signs

Looking for shapes can be an enjoyable pastime. You can limit the search to road signs or broaden it to include buildings, bridges, and other objects. The child must name the shape in order to score; for example, "I see a stop sign. It's an octagon," or "I see a school crossing sign. It's a pentagon." Octagons, rhombuses (diamonds), squares, rectangles, triangles, and circles are in plentiful supply while traveling. Children quickly learn the names of these various shapes. Here are two variations on the road sign game you can play.

Variation 1:   Each person chooses a favorite shape and counts the road signs of that shape. After a set amount of time, everyone compares their counts to see which shapes are used most frequently.

Variation 2:   Are there more red, green, or yellow road signs?

Caution: Most young children have a difficult time with competition and, in particular, with losing. Try to keep these games from becoming too competitive by focusing on the informational aspect. For example, introduce this game by saying, "It would be interesting to know if we're seeing more yellow, green, or red signs," rather than, "You pick one color and I'll pick another and we'll see who finds the most."

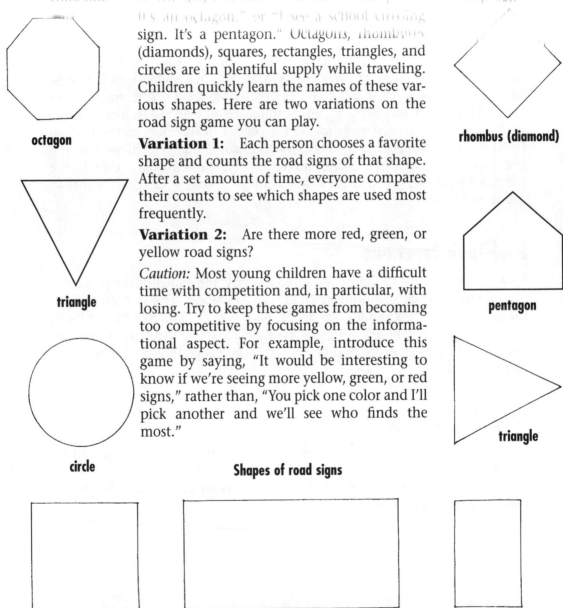

octagon

rhombus (diamond)

triangle

pentagon

circle

triangle

Shapes of road signs

rectangle (square)

rectangle

rectangle

Number Game

You can make a game of finding consecutive numbers on buildings, signs, and license plates as you look out the car window. You are only allowed to use a number when you are ready for it. (If you find a 13 when you're on 9, it doesn't count.) How far you go will depend, of course, on the ability of your passengers to read numbers. This is a good way to learn to read numbers in the teens, often a stumbling block for young children for whom 14 *sounds* as if it starts with a four.

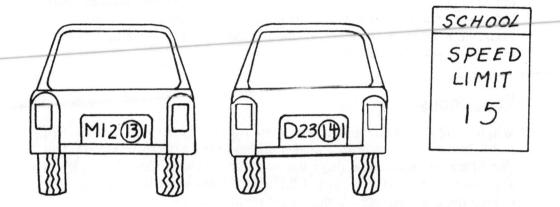

Finding consecutive numbers

Counting Cars

Counting the cars you pass is lively sport and a good cooperative game. It is also excellent practice for counting both forward and backward. You count forward when you pass a car, but you must count backward when cars pass you.

License Plates

Keep a record of the states for which you see license plates. Even if young followers are unable to read the names of the states, they will be able to spot the different colors and pictures on the plates and, in time, recognize the states they are from. Keep looking for new codes to increase the count. You may find all 50 if your trip is long enough.

Car Colors

Run a consumer research project on car color. What colors seem to be the most popular? The least popular? If you are traveling in ranch or farm country, you can play this game with the color of horses. A more complicated game would be to research car makes or models. Are there more vans, four-door sedans, or two-door coupes?

Road Maps

Map reading is a very important skill. Share your road map with the children, highlighting your route with a marker and indicating places where you will stop along the way. Show them the direction arrow, noting that north is always toward the top of the map. Children may enjoy having their own map to keep track of their journey, bringing it up to date at each stop.

At the Grocery Store

The grocery store is a treasure house of math experiences waiting to happen. But shopping at the end of the day with young children can try the patience and stamina of even the most conscientious of math-minded parents. Pick just one or two things to think about on any given trip.

The Shopping List

Compile a shopping list with your children and count all the items. Give each child a short sublist of items to select from the shelves and put in the cart.

Weight

Many items are sold by the pound, such as butter or margarine. Holding one of these items is a good way for a child to experience exactly how heavy a pound is.

Many stores have scales so that customers can weigh the produce they select. It is fun for children to hold an item in each hand—a tomato, for example, or a bunch of broccoli—and estimate which handful weighs more. Help them weigh the items to check their guesses. Estimating, as well as learning to use a scale, are useful math skills. Terms such as *most, least, more, less, heavier,* and *lighter* are important weight terms to know.

Quantity

Most grocery items are sold by quantity. Use quantifying terms and encourage children to use them as well: a *gallon, half gallon,* or *quart* of milk; a *liter* of soda; a *dozen* eggs; a *half pound* or *pound* of pasta; a *6-ounce* (170-*g*) can of tomato paste. Children will learn by checking out the numbers and the sizes on containers and, in the case of weight terminology, by experimenting with how heavy these items are when held.

Money

The grocery store is a natural place to begin learning about money, but there are pitfalls. Whole-dollar amounts and paper money are at first much easier for young children to deal with than the various coins. Adding $1 to $5 is simple compared to adding a dime, a quarter, a nickel, and a penny. However, children's first experience with money is usually with coins, and here there are a number of false clues to trip up the young learner. The penny and dime are almost the same size, except the dime is a little thinner—and worth ten times as much. The nickel is much bigger than the dime but worth half as much.

Learning the names of the coins is an additional step. Yet the names, once learned, do not provide easy clues to the cent amounts. And in dealing with coins, although one is usually dealing with smaller amounts of money, the numbers are often larger. Take on this teaching a little piece at a time.

Having money to spend is one of the best incentives to learning about money. Try giving your child just one kind of coin, perhaps starting with a certain amount in pennies.

Familiarize children with the signs $ and ¢.

Calculators

Children love to use calculators, and learning how to use one is an invaluable math skill. On days when you have purchased only a few items, help your child practice using the calculator by checking the receipt. Explain how one always begins by pressing C for clear to be sure that all earlier information has been erased. Show how the decimal point comes between the dollars and cents.

For example, "We spent $1.83 for grapes, so press the 1 key, the decimal key, the 8, and then the 3." Talk through the addition process as you demonstrate the use of the + (plus) and = (equal) keys. When you have entered all the items on the receipt, you might say, "To find out how much we spent altogether, press the equal key." Calculators are discussed at greater length in chapter 1.

Estimating Time

Children can become familiar with durations of time in relation to trips to the store through the following kinds of dialogue:

"Let's make this one a quick trip. We just need milk and some vegetables. Let's see if we can be out of here in ten minutes."

"We have a long list today. We're going to see if we can do the shopping for the whole week. I wonder how long it will take us?"

Collect estimates and see how close they come.

At the Beach

Volume

In the beach bag, be sure to bring pails and containers of various sizes and shapes. Include a measuring cup as well. Young children learn a great deal about volume in their play, just by using one container to fill another. They refine their ability to judge which container holds the most. They might discover, for example, that a taller container does not necessarily hold the largest volume of sand or water. They may become better able to make accurate estimates of how many cups of water it takes to fill a pail or how many pails of sand it takes to fill a hole.

Float or Sink?

Children can collect objects, such as sticks of various shapes and sizes, feathers, shells, pebbles, or stones, and experiment with which ones float and which ones sink. Let your child put items that float in one pile and items that sink in another. The two piles can then be compared.

Area

Children can draw pictures in the sand with a stick and "color" them in with colored stones or shells. In laying out the stones and covering a surface with them, children can explore the relationship between solid shapes and how they fit together to cover a surface. They may wish to count how many stones or shells it takes, as well.

**"Coloring" a sand drawing
of a whale with stones or shells**

Skipping Stones

Children enjoy collecting flat stones for "skipping" through the water and counting how many times they are able to make them skip. Even a child who has not yet learned to skip stones can still count skips for others who can.

Sorting According to Length

Young beachcombers can collect sticks, sort them, and line them up according to length. In doing this, children focus on one property: length. Through trial and error, they line sticks up, learn the relationship between them, and decide on placement. Of course, children can sort using other criteria, such as color, shape, or texture.

The Long Jump

The beach is a perfect place to practice the long jump. Draw a starting line and mark where your young athlete lands. Then pull out your measuring tape and help measure the length of the jump. In measuring objects with young children, it is important to show them how to line up the tape so that the beginning of the object being measured is lined up with the beginning of the tape.

Patterns

Children can look for patterns in the sand: patterns of gulls' feet, patterns of their own feet, tide marks and ripple effects or patterns etched by the wind.

AT SPORTING EVENTS

These poems describe some of the math ideas that are to be found in spectator sports. Your child may enjoy hearing them read.

FOOTBALL

The playing field's a rectangle.
The football's an ellipse.
A parallel line for each five yards,
The forty's where they kick.

One center and four backs,
Two tackles, ends, and guards,
That makes how many players?
Four tries to make ten yards.

No kick on a fourth down,
Can make a hero or a cad.
Three things can happen with a pass
And two of them are bad.

Sometimes a pass is thrown too long,
Sometimes it's thrown too wide.
Sometimes it's caught by someone
Whom you hope is on your side.

Three points for every field goal.
Each touchdown equals six.
Add one point more to the score,
When the kicker makes the kick.

—Kate Morrison

BASKETBALL

Time is a very important dimension.
It adds to the challenge, the skill, and the tension.

You'll keep track of the score with remarkable ease,
If you practice skip counting by twos and by threes.

—Kate Morrison

BASEBALL

First base, second, third, and home,
The bases number four.
Make a journey 'round a diamond,
Touch home plate to score.

Nine innings and nine players,
Three strikes, four balls, three outs.
A lot of talk to umpires,
Boos and cheers and shouts.

Numbers on the players' shirts,
Numbers in the score,
RBIs and other stats,
That make up baseball lore.

—Kate Morrison

Chapter 5

Animal Facts and Figures

W hat animal's the tallest? The smallest?
The largest overallest?

The heaviest? The lightest?
The darkest and the brightest?

The biggest teeth? The longest nose?
The largest feet? The fewest toes?

The furriest? The thinnest hair?
(You're doing math when you compare.)

—Kate Morrison

Making comparisons is a child's first experience with measurement. Ideas of more, less, heavier, lighter, longer, shorter, and equal to are precursors to an understanding of standard units of measure.

Animals, a favorite topic for many children, present numerous concepts. This chapter contains 13 sections about animals that can be read by you and your child together, one section at a time, over a period of two or three weeks—perhaps at bedtime. As the stories recall, animals come in many shapes and sizes and exhibit a multitude of different behaviors. The weight, height, number of toes and feet, and speed of various animals are given to help children compare their own characteristics with those of the animals. In doing so, children are not only working with mathematics but also learning more about the differences between people and other animals.

How Many Feet?

Feet

Feet of snails
are only one.
Birds grow two
to hop and run.
Dogs and cats
and cows grow four.
Ants and beetles
add two more.
Spiders run around on eight,
which may seem
a lot, but wait—
centipedes
have more than thirty
feet to wash
when they get dirty.

—Aileen Fisher

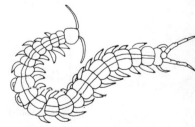

Can you think of any animals with no feet?

Centipede means "100 feet," but some centipedes have only 30 feet, while others have more than 300. Have you ever wondered how they decide which foot goes after which?

If you are interested in knowing more about feet and why they come in different shapes and sizes, you may like to read: *What Neat Feet!* by Hana Machotka, (New York: Morrow Junior Books, 1991). Also, aquariums and zoos are great places to count feet.

There are animals with 10 feet, like crabs and lobsters, and animals with 14 feet, like wood lice.

Count the feet on this caterpillar.

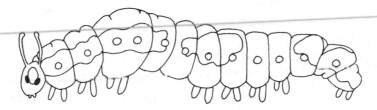

How many feet does it have when it changes into a butterfly?

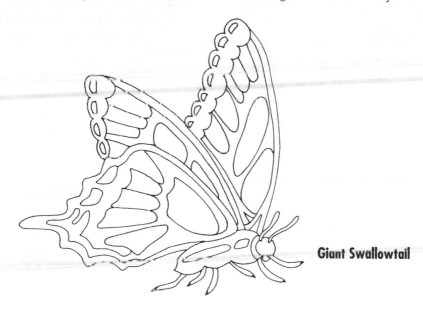

Giant Swallowtail

How many feet do you have?

How Many Toes?

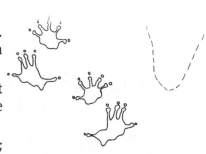

An ostrich, a bullfrog, an opossum, a hippopotamus, and a heron went for a walk. Look at the footprints they left behind.

Both the ostrich and the heron are birds. They walk on two legs. The ostrich is huge. Can you find its footprints?

Can you find the footprints of the bullfrog? It has four toes on each of its front feet and five toes on each of its back feet.

The hippopotamus has four toes on each foot; so does the heron. Which footprints belong to the hippopotamus and which belong to the heron?

Which animal has the most toes?

Which animal has the fewest toes?

If you walked on all fours like the bullfrog, opossum, and hippopotamus, your hands would be your front feet. How many toes would you have?

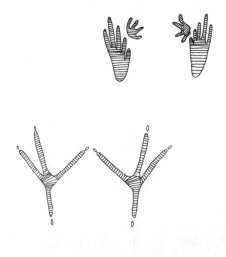

WHICH ANIMALS ARE SMALLEST?

All of the pictures you see here—except for that of the dinosaur, of course—are life-size. They are some of the smallest animals in the world today. Are they longer or shorter than your longest finger?

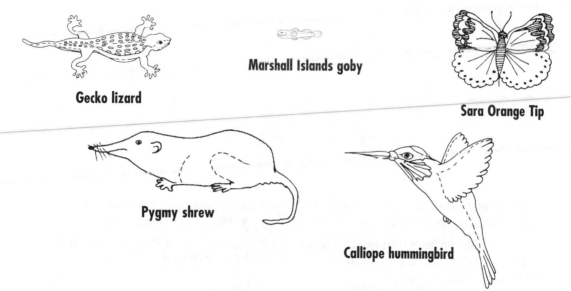

Marshall Islands goby

Gecko lizard

Sara Orange Tip

Pygmy shrew

Calliope hummingbird

One of the smallest dinosaurs, compsognathus, was just 2 feet (0.6 m) long. Was it longer than you are tall?

Compsognathus

HOW WIDE CAN YOU STRETCH YOUR ARMS?

Pteranodon

The pteranodon, a flying reptile that lived in the age of dinosaurs, had a wingspan of about 27 feet (8 m). That's about as long as two small cars.

The American white pelican has a wingspan of about 9 feet (2.7 m), and the peregrine falcon has a wingspan of about 3 feet (0.9 m).

Peregrine falcon

American white pelican

What is your arm span?

DO YOU HAVE MORE TEETH THAN AN ANTEATER?

Let's hope so. An anteater has no teeth.

A 17-foot (5-m)-long whale (that's about as long as a medium-size car) has at most four teeth.

A lunar dove snail is only as long as this line ——. It also has four teeth.

Gophers, rats, porcupines, and squirrels have about 20 teeth.

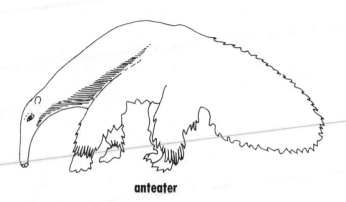

anteater

Armadillos, weasels, bats, cats, and deer have about 30 teeth. That's about the same number that you'll have when you're an adult. You'll have 32 teeth.

A crocodile has at least 60 teeth for chewing on the large animals it sometimes eats for dinner.

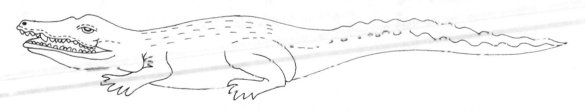

crocodile

Dolphins have about 40 teeth on each side of their upper and lower jaws. That makes 160 teeth in all. Can you imagine how long it would take a dolphin to brush its teeth at night?

How many teeth do you have now? Who has more teeth, you or a porcupine?

WHO WON THE 100-METER DASH?

Did you know that a cat can run faster than a human being? So can a fox, an ostrich, an elephant, and lots of other animals. A cheetah is the fastest animal on land. It can run faster than cars are allowed to travel on the highway.

The tortoise is one of the slowest animals. Over a thousand years ago in ancient Greece, a man called Aesop told an amazing fable about a race between a tortoise and a hare:

THE TORTOISE AND THE HARE

The Hare could run very fast and often laughed at the slow pace of other animals, especially the Tortoise. The Tortoise challenged the Hare to a race. The Hare thought that this was ridiculous. It would be impossible for the Tortoise to beat him.

The race began and the Tortoise plodded along, never stopping to look around. The Hare was so sure of winning that after running a little, he decided to take a nap. When he finally woke up, he was furious to see that the Tortoise had already crossed the finish line.

Imagine that the race was the 100-meter dash. That's about the length of a football field. It would take the Hare about 5 seconds to run from one end of a football field to the other. Clap your hands slowly five times. That's about 5 seconds. It would take the Tortoise a little over a half hour to go from one end to the other. That's about as long as it takes to clap your hands 1,800 times. Don't you think that the Hare should have first run the race and then taken a nap? How far can you run in 5 seconds?

The fastest human being can run the 100-meter dash in a little over 9 seconds. That's about as along as it takes to clap your hands ten times. How long would it take you to run the 100-meter dash?

If you had a race with the Tortoise and the Hare, who do you think would win?

How Many Gallons of Milk Do You Weigh?

Ten pennies weigh about 1 ounce (28 g). Hold ten pennies in your hand. Do you think they're light? That's how much the pygmy shrew weighs.

A pygmy shrew weighs about the same as ten pennies.

A hamster weighs about 4 ounces (112 g). That's the same as 40 pennies. Hold 40 pennies in your hand. Do they feel heavy or light? That's how much a hamster weighs.

One gallon (4 liters) of milk weighs about 8 pounds (4 kg). A large rabbit weighs about the same as a gallon of milk.

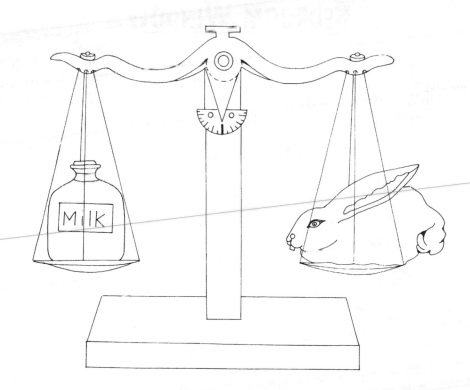

A rabbit weighs about the same as a gallon of milk.

A Doberman Pinscher weighs about the same as 10 gallons of milk. That's 80 pounds (40 kg).

About how many gallons (liters) of milk do you weigh?

Suppose you weigh 36 pounds (16 kg). That's 8 pounds + 8 pounds + 8 pounds + 8 pounds + 4 pounds. You would weigh the same as 4½ gallons (18 liters) of milk.

COULD A GIRAFFE LOOK INTO YOUR BEDROOM WINDOW?

Suppose you are in your bedroom on the second floor of your house. A gorilla, an elephant, and a giraffe come to visit. A gorilla is about 5 feet (1.5 m) tall; an elephant, about 13 feet (4 m) tall; and a giraffe, about 17 feet (5.2 m) tall. Which of the animals could see into your bedroom window?

Meters

Feet

HOW MANY PEOPLE ARE IN YOUR FAMILY?

Human families come in all sizes and combinations. It's the same with animals. Some animals like to live together in large families; others live in smaller families or even prefer to be on their own.

Rhinoceroses like to be alone, except when a mother has a baby cub. They stay together till the cub is about five years old. Sometimes a few rhinoceroses will get together and wallow in the mud.

Both gorillas and elephants live in families of about ten. The difference is that in the gorilla families, there are adult males and females and children. In the elephant families, all the grownups are females. Male elephants live on their own or sometimes in groups with other males.

There are usually five or six wolves in a family: a mother, a father, and two or three cubs.

Dolphins have very large families. It is not unusual to see forty dolphins swimming together.

How many people are there in your family? You can count just the people who live with you, or grandparents, aunts, uncles, and cousins as well.

How many giraffes in this family?

DOES A GIRAFFE GET A GOOD NIGHT'S SLEEP?

Can you imagine spending most of your day, like a giraffe, looking for food, eating it, and looking for more food? There would be no time to go to school, play with your friends, read, or watch even one show on television. After spending many hours looking for food, giraffes lie down at about midnight and digest their food for a few hours, catching a few minutes of sleep at a time. Altogether, they get only 20 minutes of sound deep sleep. That's about as long as it takes you to play a game of checkers or eat a meal.

Giraffes do rest during the day, but usually they remain standing. If they sit down, they still keep their necks upright and don't keep their eyes closed for long. They're always on the lookout for other animals that might want to harm them.

Elephants also don't seem to need much sleep. They go to sleep at midnight and wake up very early in the morning, when they start to look for food. What time do you go to bed at night? Have you ever gone to sleep at midnight?

A giraffe sleeping deeply

Nocturnal animals sleep during the day and are awake at night. Raccoons rise around sunset. They spend a few hours looking for a place that has their favorite foods—berries, seeds, nuts, crabs, and crayfish. They eat until about three o'clock in the morning. Then, they go home and fall asleep as the sun is rising.

Some animals are asleep more than they're awake. Gorillas build nests on the ground at sunset and then sleep for about 13 hours. After they wake up early the next morning, they look for food. Then, they rest, sleep, and play until it's time to go to bed again. What time do you wake up in the morning?

Lions love to sleep. They sleep at night, and they also take a lot of catnaps during the day. They can sometimes sleep for a total of 20 hours a day. That's like going to sleep at eight o'clock at night, sleeping through breakfast and lunch, and only waking up for an afternoon snack. Do you take a nap during the day? How many hours a day do you sleep?

A rhinoceros sleeps for about 9 hours at night. Do you sleep more or less than a rhinoceros?

A beluga whale has the strangest sleeping routine. Only half of its body sleeps at a time. One side of its brain is awake while the other is asleep. Then the other side takes a turn. You can tell it's half asleep because it keeps one eye open. See if you can go to sleep with one eye open.

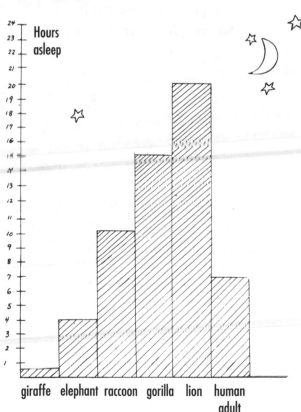

The number of hours per day that different animals spend sleeping

Hours asleep

giraffe elephant raccoon gorilla lion human adult

WHO EATS MORE, YOU OR A MASKED SHREW?

Elephants eat about 400 pounds (182 kg) of food a day. That's like eating 800 bananas—that's about one banana for each minute that you're awake.

Crocodiles only eat about once a week. But then, they can eat a whole animal without sharing it with any of their friends. So, if you ate like a crocodile, you'd eat one huge meal on Monday and not eat anything again until the next Monday.

A masked shrew eats insects, snails, and worms all day long. The amount of food it eats weighs more than the shrew itself. This tiny animal is about the same size as the picture.

If you were to eat as much as you weigh, you would have to eat about 160 quarter–pound hamburgers in one day.

So, who do you think eats more, you or a masked shrew?

masked shrew

When it comes to drinking, a giraffe drinks about 20 gallons (76 liters) of water a day. An elephant drinks about the same amount.

How much do you drink each day? To find out, choose a day—perhaps one day over the weekend—and count how many glasses of juice, milk, water, or other liquids you drink.

WHO WON THE LONG-JUMP COMPETITION?

Imagine that a flea, a jumping mouse, a frog, Mike Powell, the 1991 long-jump champion, and a kangaroo are going to have a long-jump competition. Can you guess who will win?

The drawings show how far each one can jump.

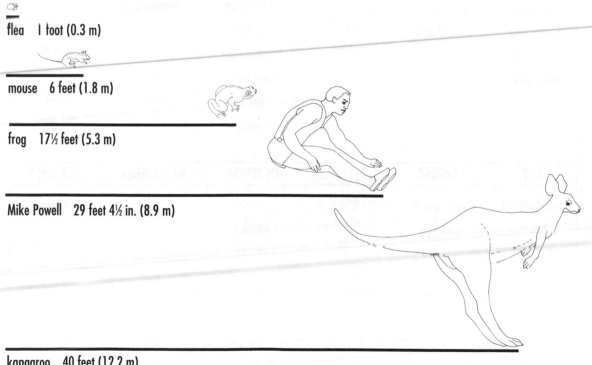

flea   1 foot (0.3 m)

mouse   6 feet (1.8 m)

frog   17½ feet (5.3 m)

Mike Powell   29 feet 4½ in. (8.9 m)

kangaroo   40 feet (12.2 m)

The kangaroo can jump the farthest. But strange as it may seem, the flea is the best jumper.

A flea is only about the size of the head of a pin, but it can jump from one end of a 12-inch (30-cm) ruler to the other in one leap. For Mike Powell to jump as far in proportion to his height, he would have to jump the length of three football fields.

How far can you jump?

WHEN WERE YOU BORN?

Did you know that some animals are born only at certain times of the year? The calendar shows the birth months of some animals.

JANUARY	FEBRUARY	MARCH	APRIL	MAY	JUNE
black bear	black bear	armadillo	armadillo	bighorn sheep	bighorn sheep
polar bear	polar bear	Washington gray squirrel	shorttail weasel	shorttail weasel	ferret
grizzly bear	hooded seal	red fox	red fox	flying squirrel	Douglas squirrel
brown bear			flying squirrel	porcupine	ground squirrel
gray seal			porcupine	bison	bison
			bison	coyote	sea lion
			coyote		

JULY	AUGUST	SEPTEMBER	OCTOBER	NOVEMBER	DECEMBER
ground squirrel	flying squirrel	flying squirrel	ocelot	ocelot	gray seal
bison	tailed frog	tailed frog	Douglas squirrel		
sea lion					

Wouldn't it be strange if people were like porcupines and had birthdays only in April and May? Do you know people born in April or May? In what month were you born? What animals are born in the same month as you? Do you know anyone born in the same months as a black bear?

Chapter 6

Crafts That Use Math

M ath concepts are central to many crafts activities. This chapter presents crafts projects for you to do with your children, grouped according to the major math ideas embedded in the projects, or the nature of the activities.

All of the projects have been used successfully with young children. The projects vary in the amount of preparation required. Some children will be able to do most of the preparatory work themselves, while others may need more assistance. Your child's age, interest, and small motor development are key factors. Let your child's interest and enjoyment be your guide to the amount of assistance needed.

Following are suggestions about some of the most commonly used materials. Besides being used for many of the projects, these materials come in handy when there are children in the house.

Construction paper   It comes in a variety of colors and is available in most art supply and stationery stores.

Glue sticks   These are easy for children to use. Show your child how to turn them up only a little (so they don't break off) and recap them (so they don't dry up).

Paper glue   Used straight from the squeeze bottle, this glue is very satisfactory for making paper constructions. Squeeze a little glue onto the surface to be glued, then press the two pieces of paper together tightly while counting slowly to ten.

Scissors   These must be of good quality for children to learn to use them with ease. Look for blunt scissors made especially for children. There are many excellent brands on the market. Left-handed scissors are also available if your child needs them.

Crayons   Crayons differ in size and in the intensity of their color. Thick crayons are easier for young children to hold.

Markers   Look for sets with nontoxic, washable ink.

SYMMETRY

Symmetry, as defined by Webster, is "balanced proportions" or "beauty of form arising from balanced proportions." Something that is symmetrical is capable of being divided into two identical halves. It is a concept linked as closely to mathematics as to art.

Children can begin experimenting with the idea of symmetry by doing art projects with folded paper. Unfolding their paper and seeing the whole design, with mirror images on either side of a center fold, is a source of great pleasure and satisfaction to young artists.

Jack-O'-Lantern

Materials: Orange construction paper, markers or crayons, and scissors.

- Fold the sheet of orange construction paper in half so that the short ends are aligned.
- Draw half of a pumpkin from top to bottom along the fold.
- Cut along the line you just drew, being sure to cut through both thicknesses of paper but not along the fold.
- Unfold the paper and decorate it with a jack-o'-lantern face.

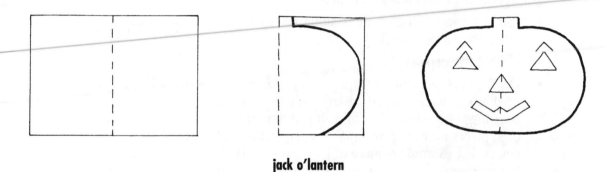

jack o'lantern

Many other simple decorations may be similarly made; for example, bats for Halloween, birds and butterflies in the spring, leaves in the fall, and hearts for Valentine's Day.

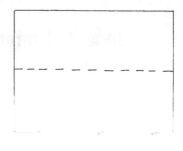

"Stained Glass" Windows

The beauty of this project is that symmetry makes any kind of squiggly cutout pleasing to the eye when the paper is unfolded. Also, your child will gain experience in combining color.

Materials: Black construction paper, scissors, glue or transparent tape, and small pieces of colored tissue paper or cellophane.

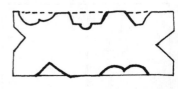

- Fold the sheet of black construction paper in half so that the long ends are aligned.
- Cut out two or three designs along the fold. Cut along the edges as well.
- Unfold the paper.
- On the back side, glue or tape small pieces of colored tissue paper or cellophane over the cutout openings. Experiment by allowing different colored pieces to overlap and make other shades and colors. For example, a piece of blue paper partially covering one of yellow will make that opening part yellow, part green.
- Tape the finished "stained glass" paper on a window. When the sun shines through the window, the effect can be dazzling.

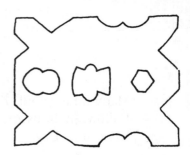

"stained glass" window

Symmetrical Painting

Materials: Paper, paintbrush, and tempera or watercolor paints.

- Fold a piece of paper in half and then unfold it.
- Paint with tempera or watercolors on half of the page.
- While the painting is still wet, fold the blank half over the painted half and press together firmly.
- Unfold the paper carefully and allow the painting to dry.

Snowflakes

Materials: Circles of thin white paper cut from typing or copier paper (flattened basket-type coffee filters are another possibility), scissors, and tape. (Optional: glue and black or brightly colored paper.)

- Fold the circle in half to form a semicircle. Fold it in half once more to form a wedge. (The more times you fold the circle, the more intricate the design of your snowflake.)

- Draw a curved line between the two corners of the unfolded edge, and then cut along this line.

- Cut small designs, such as semicircles and triangles, around all three edges of the wedges. If you cut off the tip of the wedge, you will have a design in the center of your snowflake as well.

- Unfold the snowflake. Then, tape it to a window or glue it onto a background of black or brightly colored paper.

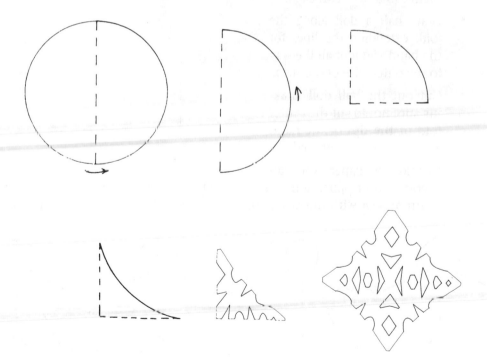

snowflake

Paper-Doll Chains

Making paper-doll chains is another activity that uses paper folding and depends, for its results, on the property of symmetry.

Materials: Scissors; 8½-by-11 inch (21.5-by-28 cm) typing or copier paper, thin enough to allow small hands to cut through many folds; and crayons or markers.

- Fold the paper in half lengthwise, and cut it into two strips 4¼ × 11 inches (11 × 28 cm) long.

- Fold one of the strips in half so that the short ends are aligned. Then, fold the strip twice more in the same direction. This will give you a pleated strip with eight panels that measure 1⅜ × 4¼ inches (3.5 × 11 cm) each.

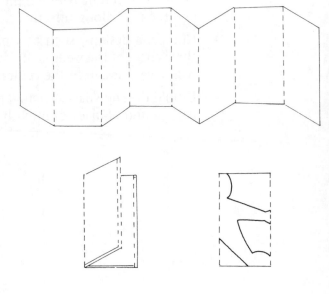

- Draw half a doll along the fold, extending the lines for the hand and foot all the way to the outer edge of the strip.

- Cut out the half doll, making sure not to cut the center fold or the tips of the hand and foot on the outer edge.

- Unfold the paper. You can decorate your paper-doll chain with crayons or markers. If you made a chain of boys with this strip, you can make a chain of girls with the other.

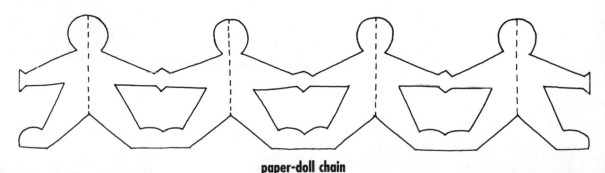

paper-doll chain

PATTERNS

Patterns are always pleasing, but what do they have to do with math? In working with patterns, whether "ready-made" or created by children themselves, children are dealing with a collection of items that have a set relationship to one another. The tasks before them are complex. In a ready-made pattern, they must determine the existing relationship and then try to duplicate it. If they are creating their own pattern, they must think of the way they want to order their material and then duplicate that.

Patterning requires children to observe carefully, to analyze what they see, and then to respond in a logical way. Such problem-solving abilities are crucial for clear mathematical thinking.

Name Patterns

Materials: Paper, ruler, and markers or crayons.

- Make a grid with squares, each of which is large enough to contain one letter of your child's handwritten name. The number of squares in a row should be at least one more than the number of letters in the name. The number of columns should be equal to the number of squares in a row.

- Write the name across the top row, starting at the top left square and placing one letter in each square.

- After completing the name, begin again in the very next square. Do not skip any squares.

- When the top row is full, continue the name on the next row. Continue writing the name until the grid is filled.

- With crayon or marker, color the first letter of the name wherever it appears on the grid. Find the pattern. Do the other letters create patterns as well?

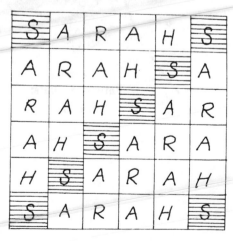

name pattern

Rubbings

Patterns are all around us—throughout our homes and in nature. It is fun to look for patterns. When you find one you like, make a rubbing of it.

Materials: Thin sturdy paper, such as typing or copier paper; and peeled crayons of various colors (Optional: transparent tape and cardboard).

- Place the paper over the pattern that is to be duplicated. If the object being duplicated is likely to move—a leaf, for example—tape it to a piece of cardboard.

- Rub the side of a peeled crayon across the paper until an image of the object appears.

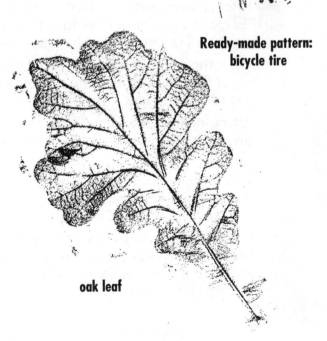

Ready-made pattern: bicycle tire

Pattern in nature: ivy leaf

oak leaf

Cereal Necklaces

Children love to string and wear colorful necklaces. Stringing a necklace can be a good exercise in patterning. The fact that these necklaces are edible is an added attraction.

Materials: A box of colored circle–shaped cereal (such as Froot Loops) and string or yarn.

- Select several pieces of the cereal and arrange them in a pattern—for example, brown, pink, green; or brown, yellow, pink, yellow, green.
- Tie the first piece of cereal to the end of the string or yarn, leaving a few inches of the string free.
- Continue to string cereal onto the necklace, repeating the pattern over and over.
- When the necklace is long enough to go over your head, tie the ends of the string together and put it on (or eat it!).

Variation: Here's an excellent opportunity to count to 100 and to experience how much 100 of something actually is. Take an egg carton or muffin tin and cover 2 of the 12 openings so that only 10 are showing. Place ten pieces of cereal in each of the ten openings. String these 100 pieces of cereal to make a necklace. How long is your 100-bead necklace?

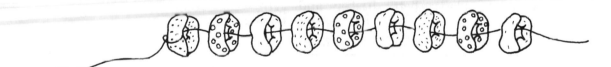

cereal necklace

WEAVING

Even the simplest and most rudimentary weaving proves to be a very satisfying experience to the young weaver. It teaches some very important basic concepts: under and over, in and out, back and forth. It is an excellent tool for developing a child's sense of direction. As children become more adept, they are able to incorporate a wide variety of color combinations, textures, and patterns.

The weaving activities that follow use four very different looms: a plastic berry basket, a paper frame, four straws, and a cardboard frame. All four activities, however, are based on the same principles: Each incorporates both the warp (that which is being woven upon) and the weft (the strands of yarn, ribbon, string, or paper that are woven in and out of the warp).

Plastic Basket Weaving

A plastic berry basket provides the basis for a simple first activity in weaving. The basket is a ready-made loom with a built-in warp. Provide your child with the weft—some thick yarn, ribbon, or strips of paper that are thin enough to slip easily in and out of the openings in the basket. If your weaver is using yarn, you may find it helpful to stiffen the end by wrapping the tip with transparent tape.

Materials: Plastic berry basket; and yarn, ribbon, or strips of paper. (Optional: colored pipe cleaners.)

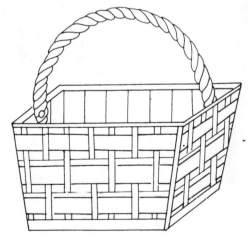

- Follow the standard weaving pattern. Starting along the bottom row on any side of the basket, weave the yarn, ribbon, or paper strip in and out of the basket openings. Continue around all four sides.

- When you get to the second row, make sure the in-and-out pattern alternates with that of the first row. The weft should come out where it went in on the first row. It takes some experience before the young weaver

woven berry basket

begins to see this alternating pattern. This can come later. Let the amount of weaving be decided by what appeals to your child.

- Tuck in all loose ends.
- Make a handle for your basket, using braided yarn or twisted pipe cleaners.

Paper Weaving

A paper weaving makes a nice place mat. It is made by weaving paper strips through slits cut in a sheet of paper. The task is made easier for young children by spacing the slits in the paper farther apart and cutting wider strips than those given in the directions.

Materials: A large sheet of construction paper, the size and color of the desired place mat; construction paper of contrasting colors; ruler; pencil; scissors; and glue. (Optional: clear Con-Tact Paper.)

- Fold the large sheet of paper in half so that the short ends are aligned.
- Use a ruler to draw lines perpendicular to the fold at 1½-inch (4-cm) intervals and ending 1½ inches (4 cm) from the opposite edge.
- Cut along these lines with scissors to make the slits (warp) through which you will weave.

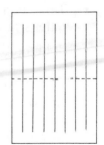

- Unfold the paper.
- Cut strips of paper (weft) of a contrasting color or colors that are 1½ inches (4 cm) wide and as long as the place mat is wide.
- Weave these strips over and under the paper slits in alternating rows.
- When no more strips will fit, ease the strips closer together and secure the ends with glue.
- If you like, cover the finished place mat with clear Con-Tact self-adhesive covering so that it can be wiped clean.

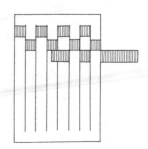

woven paper place mat

Weaving on Straws

Ordinary plastic straws can become a loom to make a belt for young weavers.

Materials: Yarn, scissors, four straws of equal length, and transparent tape.

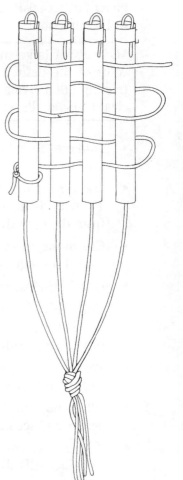

- Cut four lengths of yarn, each of which is twice the waist measurement of the recipient of the belt.

- Thread one of the lengths of yarn through each straw, and secure the end of the yarn to the top of the straw with tape. (An easy way to thread a straw, if you are not averse to a mouthful of yarn, is to insert one end of the yarn in the bottom of the straw and suck the yarn up through the straw.)

- Tie the free ends of the four lengths of yarn together in a loose knot, 2 to 3 inches (5 to 7.5 cm) from the end. These lengths of yarn form the warp.

- To begin weaving, cut another length of yarn. A manageable size is the length of your child's out-stretched arms (about 1 yard or 1 meter). This yarn will be the weft.

- Tie one end of the weft yarn around one of the outer straws.

- Holding the straws flat in one hand, begin to weave the weft yarn over and under, back and forth across the straws, working toward the outer end of the straws. As you weave more weft yarn onto the straws, push down what you've already woven to make more working space at the top. This can be easily done by holding the woven portion in one hand and gently pulling each of the four straws up.

- When the first length of the weft yarn has been woven, cut another length and tie it to the end of the first. Continue weaving as before.

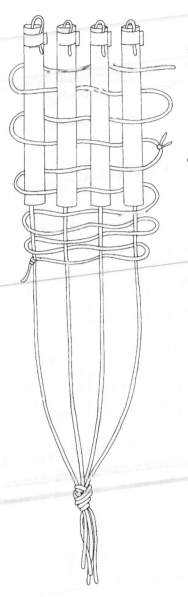

- As the woven yarn begins to fill the straw loom, move this woven portion gently down onto the warp yarn that projects from the bottom of the straws.

- Check from time to time to determine when the weaving is long enough to go around the recipient's waist. When it's the right length, carefully push the rest of the weaving off the straws and onto the warp yarns, making sure the warp yarns do not pull out of the straws prematurely.

- Center the weaving on the warp yarns so that there are equal amounts of unwoven warp at each end. Detach the warp yarns from the straws. Untie the loose knot made earlier, then tie the warp yarns securely together with a knot at either side of the weaving to form tassels.

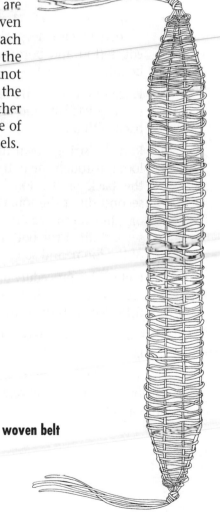

woven belt

Weaving on a Cardboard Loom

A simple loom can be made out of cardboard and string.

TO MAKE THE LOOM

Materials: Ruler; scissors; a piece of stiff cardboard (poster board or cardboard from an old carton); and a ball of stout string.

- Cut a piece of cardboard to measure 6 × 9 inches (15 × 23 cm).

- Make slits ⅜ inch (1 cm) apart and ⅜ inch (1 cm) deep along the short edges (top and bottom) of the cardboard.

- Place one end of the ball of string in the top left slit, and anchor it to the back with a knot.

- Run the string down the front of the loom, through the bottom left slit, up the back of the loom, through the second slit at the top, down the front of the loom again, through the second slit at the bottom, up the back of the loom, and so on.

- Follow this procedure until all the slits are filled and the entire loom is threaded with the warp.

- Cut the string and secure it with a knot.

Use one side of your newly constructed cardboard loom to weave a miniature rug or blanket.

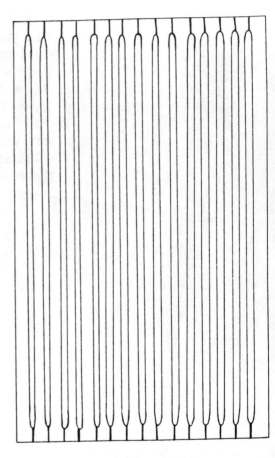

cardboard loom

TO WEAVE A MINIATURE RUG OR BLANKET

Materials: Scissors; yarn in a variety of bright colors; and your cardboard loom.

- Cut some yarn (weft), about the length of your outstretched arms, and tie it onto one of the outer warp strings.

- Begin weaving loosely—over and under, back and forth across the loom—being especially careful to encircle the outer warp strings each time you change direction.

- Tie each new length of weft yarn to the end of the preceding one.

- Continue with the weaving until it is the desired length.

TO FINISH OFF THE WEAVING

- Ease the weaving to the center of the loom.

- Cut the warp strings at top and bottom.

- Tie pairs of adjacent warp strings together in square knots until all loose strings are tied.

DRAWING

What does drawing have to do with mathematics? In drawing these pictures, children are learning to follow directions, step by step. In the process, they are learning about manipulating line segments, open and closed curves, two-dimensional shapes, and space. You may want to read the accompanying poems aloud as your child experiments with the drawings.

How to Draw an Elephant

Draw an arch,

Add a dome,

An ear,

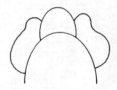

Another ear,

A squiggle tail,

Some feet,

A trunk.

An elephant—from the rear.

—Kate Morrison

How to Draw a Duck

Draw a slice of watermelon
Balancing in space.

A triangle with squiggles
Puts wings in proper place.

Draw head and neck

 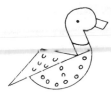

And then a beak.

Add two legs

And webbed feet.

—Kate Morrison

How to Draw a Stegosaurus

Start off with a wavy line.

Mountain peaks beneath.

Add two spikes, a head, an eye,

A smile to hide its teeth.

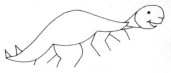

Legs in back, legs in front.

Be sure to give it feet.

Pentagons upon its back,

And add some plants to eat.

—Kate Morrison

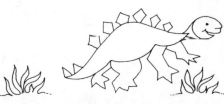

TESSELLATIONS

A tessellation is a mosaic. Like a jigsaw puzzle, it is made up of geometric shapes that fit neatly into each other, with no spaces between. However, unlike a jigsaw puzzle, each piece of a tessellation is identical in shape. These shapes can be quite complex. They are made according to mathematical rules and have fascinated people of all ages, artists and mathematicians alike. Looking at a book of tessellations by the artist M. C. Escher is a good way to spark interest.

Materials: Cardboard, scissors, pencil, transparent tape, and crayons or markers.

- Below are some simple shapes that tessellate. Trace them onto a piece of cardboard and cut them out to use as templates.

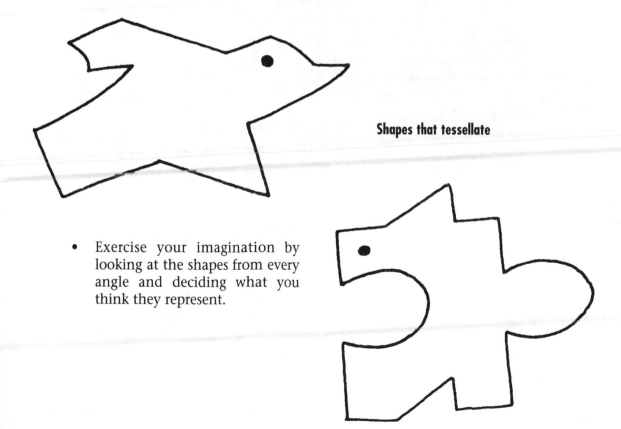

Shapes that tessellate

- Exercise your imagination by looking at the shapes from every angle and deciding what you think they represent.

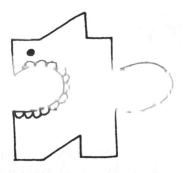

- Draw around one of the shapes again and again, fitting the tracings against each other with no spaces between. As you draw, notice the properties of the shape—how its edges fit together, and how you can line up tracing after tracing to cover a surface. (At first, children may need some help to make sure they have lined up the template accurately. A little tape, lightly applied, will keep the template in place while it is being traced.)

- When the page is full—or as full as desired—the individual tracings of the tessellation can be colored with crayons or markers.

PAPER CONSTRUCTIONS

For the following paper constructions, children fold and cut paper into rectangles, squares, triangles, circles, semicircles and arches. They learn to distinguish between the long and short ends of the paper, and between the folded and the outer edges. They become familiar with terms such as *top, bottom, width,* and *length.* They learn to fold on the diagonal, and in half, and to glue strips of paper at right angles. They explore all these things while making creations that delight them, and they learn not by memorizing terms but by getting involved in projects that they enjoy.

Paper Airplane

To make a plane that will glide through the air, begin with a rectangular sheet of paper. An ordinary sheet of typing or copier paper works well.

Materials: A sheet of typing or copier paper.

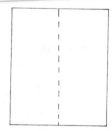

- Fold the paper in half so that the long ends are together (in a hot dog bun shape). Make a firm crease.

- Unfold the paper. The fold divides the sheet into two rectangles, each of which is half the size of the paper.

- Fold each of the two bottom corners toward the crease so that the corners touch each other. The folded-back corners form two right-angle triangles.

- Fold the base (folded edge) of each right-angle triangle to the center crease to create two larger triangles.

- Fold the plane in half again along the original crease so that the folded triangles are on the inside.

- Fold the edges opposite the center fold back toward the center fold to make the wings. The plane is ready to launch.

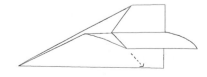

Paper Cat

Materials. One piece of black 9 by 12 inch (22 by 30 cm) construction paper, scissors, glue, and a small piece of contrasting colored paper.

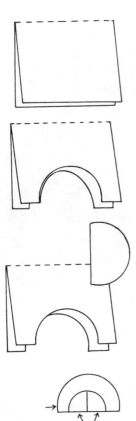

- Fold the piece of black paper in half so that the short ends are aligned.

- Keeping the paper folded, cut a large semicircle through both thicknesses of paper on the edge opposite the fold, leaving uncut about 1 inch (2.5 cm) at each end to form the legs. This folded piece is the body.

- Glue one of the semicircles you have cut out onto the outside of the cat's body above one pair of legs. This semicircle is the cat's head.

- Cut a slightly smaller semicircle out of the remaining semicircle. Cut this smaller semicircle in half to make the cat's ears. The thin arch that remains is for the cat's tail.

- Glue the tail to the end of the body opposite the head, and glue the ears to the top of the head.

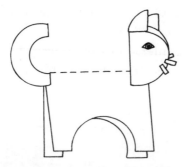

- Cut an eye and some whiskers out of brightly colored paper, and glue them onto the head also.

Paper Springs

Children love to make paper springs. They can be used to decorate the inside of greeting cards, so that objects like hearts and heads pop up when the card is opened. Springs can also be used as arms and legs of puppets.

Materials: Scissors; construction paper of any color; and tape, glue, a stapler, or for greater mobility, brads.

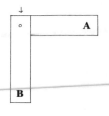

- Cut out two strips of construction paper, each of which is 1 inch (2.5 cm) wide and twice as long as you would like the finished spring to be.

- Using tape, glue, a stapler, or brads, fasten the two strips together at one end so that they are at right angles to one another.

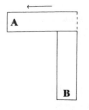

- Fold the bottom strip (A) back across the top strip (B) so that they remain at right angles to one another.

- Fold the bottom strip (B) up across the top strip (A).

- Continue folding the bottom strip over the top strip until all the paper is used and the spring is ready for action.

To decorate a greeting card: Glue the bottom of the spring to the inside of the card. Then make a heart or face, and glue it to the top of the spring. When the card is closed, the spring folds up. When it is opened again, the spring pops out.

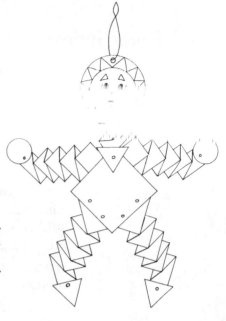

To make a puppet: Use springs for the arms, legs, and neck. Cut different shapes—circles or squares, rectangles, triangles, or rhombuses (diamonds)—in various sizes for the head, body, hands, and feet. Punch a hole near the top of the head. Run a piece of string through it and tie the ends together. Your puppet will dance as you jiggle the string.

puppet

Paper Chains

Materials: Scissors, paper in a variety of colors and textures, and glue.

Paper chains, dangling or looped across a room, lend themselves to numerous possibilities as decoration. Some children enjoy linking their paper circles together in color patterns. Others prefer a more random approach.

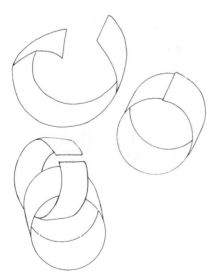

- Cut out thin strips of paper. The chain will be more interesting if you vary the length, width, and color of the paper strips. Cut some with straight edges and some with wavy edges.

- Glue together the two ends of the first strip to make a loop.

- Run the second strip through the first loop, and glue its ends together to make two interlinked loops.

- Proceed in this manner, linking loops until the chain is the desired length.

Paper-Bag Masks

The mask activity described below is for decorative masks rather than masks to wear. However, it is always possible to cut holes for eyes if children want to wear their masks.

paper in a variety
aint, and markers.

ery bag (with no
side only) makes a
the construction
aps into different
icircles, triangles,
and rhombuses
variety of sizes.
cutting out shapes
h they may need
trace around or
the paper by an

completely open.
the mask to make a
better. It is a good
ild experiment and
e placement of the
before finally gluing
ter the shapes are in
ishing touches with
glitter, if desired.

PILLOWS

In making a small pillow, children practice measuring with a ruler or tape measure. They improve their sense of direction and their ability to think in terms of in and out, while sewing around the perimeter of a square, rectangle or circle. Be sure to offer lots of help with cutting, pinning, and using sharp needles.

Materials: Ruler or tape measure; scissors; soft, colorful fabric; dressmaker's pins; tailor's chalk; needle and thread; cotton batting or other stuffing (old pairs of nylon pantyhose, cut into small pieces, are washable and make good pillow stuffing).

- Decide what size and shape you want the pillow to be.
- Measure and cut two pieces of material that are the same size.
- Pin the two pieces of material together so that the right sides of the fabric are facing each other.
- Draw stitching guide lines along three edges of the material. The fourth edge is not sewn at this time.
- Sew around the three marked edges of the pillow, in and out in a running stitch. (It is easier for young children to manage sewing tasks if the thread has been doubled, although this makes for a little more trouble when the thread gets knotted or tangled.) Tie the thread.

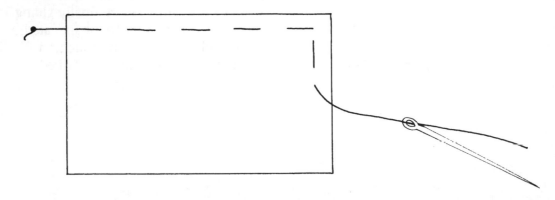

How to make a running stitch

- Turn the pillow inside out and stuff it loosely. Pin the fourth side shut, tucking the rough edges under.
- Sew the fourth side of the pillow closed in either a running or overcast stitch. Tie the thread, and the pillow is finished.

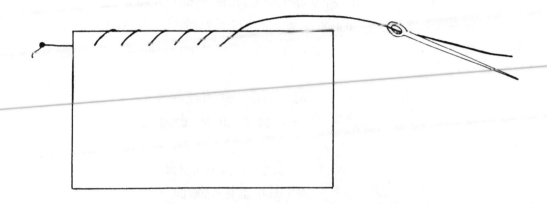

How to make an overcast stitch

MARSHMALLOW FUN

Marshmallow Fun

No doubt you've been told not to play with your food.
Though sometimes it's rude, it can also be good.
Marshmallows plus toothpicks plus imagination
Can add up to hours of recreation.

Sides, joints, segments, lines,
Patterns, points, shapes, designs.

Make a star. Make a stair.
Build a castle in the air.

Make a tepee. Make a tower.
There's no end to toothpick power.

And when you think your work's completed,
Let it harden—or just eat it.

—Kate Morrison

Playing with toothpicks and marshmallows provides a way for children to build shapes and become familiar with their geometric properties. For example, they may begin to notice that a triangle is made with three toothpicks and three marshmallows, a square with four of each. They may see that they can build a pyramid from either a square base or a triangular base. They may come to realize that cubes collapse easily and are made stronger when reinforced with a diagonal toothpick. As they work with various geometric shapes and talk about them, they will begin to integrate what they are learning.

Materials: For each of these activities, you will need a large bag of miniature-marshmallows or gumdrops and a box of round toothpicks.

Making Random Shapes

Spread the marshmallows and toothpicks out and give your child the opportunity to build any lines or shapes desired.

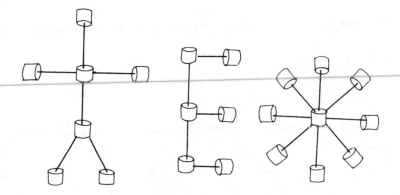

Making Shapes with Triangles and Squares

After a time, your child can make triangles and squares, then connect them to make new shapes.

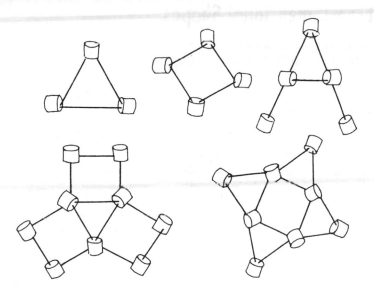

Making Many-Sided Figures

Children also enjoy building shapes that get bigger and bigger.

Help your child build pentagons, hexagons, heptagons, octagons, nonagons, decagons, dodecagons, and many more. Children love learning these names. The more sides the figure has, the closer it comes to looking like a circle.

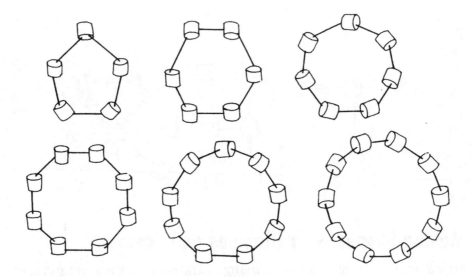

Making Three-Dimensional Shapes

Three–dimensional shapes are a challenge. Use gumdrops, or allow the marshmallows to harden just a little before working with them.

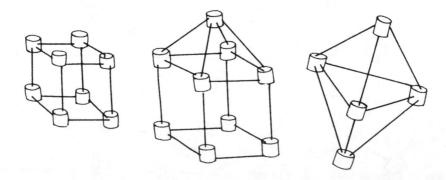

Playing Shape Games

Children can play games with shapes. The first player builds a triangle, the second player builds a triangle off the first one, and so on. See if the table can be covered with triangles. The game can also be played with hexagons, a combination of octagons and squares, or a combination of triangles and squares.

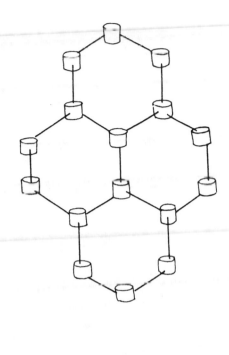

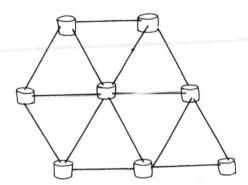

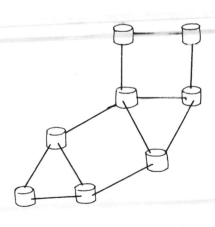

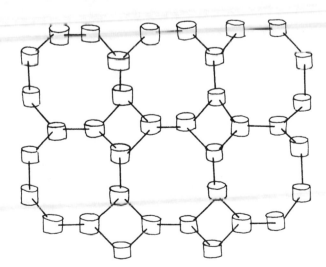

Chapter 7

Games and Math

Play is the business of young children. Games and puzzles are a natural medium in which much learning can take place. Some games provide an opportunity to exercise logic and strategy; others are mainly games of chance. Children come to recognize the difference between these types of games.

A big step in a child's development is to learn to play games bound by rules. Young children prefer to make up rules as they go along, so playing a game fairly is often difficult for them to accept.

It is therefore important to be aware that, though winning or losing can add zest to a game, many young players feel defeated or discouraged by a loss.

Try to minimize the win/lose aspect and concentrate instead on the pleasure of playing together. The spirit in which these games are played is at least as important as the math learning that occurs.

Games can provide opportunities for the development of many different skills and concepts. Card games, for example, involve sorting by number or letter; recognizing and writing numbers; comparing numbers by values of greater than, less than, or equal to; counting to determine which player has the most or fewest cards; or dealing out an equal number of cards at the beginning of the game.

Some games, such as tangrams, involve an understanding of two-dimensional shapes. Outdoor games like hopscotch reinforce mathematical ideas at the same time that they provide children with an opportunity to develop physical skills through active movement.

Playing with mathematical ideas gives children a love of, and comfort with math that no amount of drill could ever provide.

Who's Going to Go First?

For many games, children have to decide who will go first, who will be "It," or who will shuffle and deal. One way to do this is to have each player roll a die. The player with the highest number goes first. You could also decide that the player with the lowest number goes first.

Rock, Paper, Scissors or Morra can also be used for this purpose, or just played on their own.

Rock, Paper, Scissors

Two people can play this game.

Players hide one hand behind their backs. At the count of three, they bring their hands out in front of them, to represent a rock, paper, or scissors.

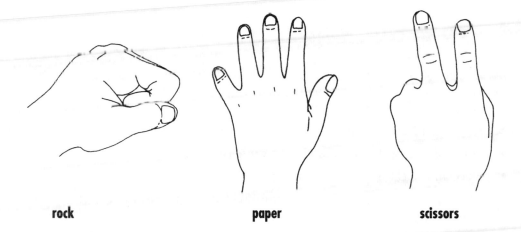

rock   paper   scissors

Scissors beats paper because scissors can cut paper. Paper beats a rock because paper can cover a rock. A rock beats scissors because a rock can make scissors dull.

For every round, the winner scores one point. Whoever is first to get a predetermined number of points wins.

Morra, or Fingers

This game is also for two people.

The object of this game is to guess the total number of fingers held up by both players.

Players start the game with a clenched fist. On the count of three, they both call out a number at the same time that they unclench their fists and hold up one, two, three, four, or five fingers. The person who correctly guessed the exact number of fingers held by both players gets a point.

The winner is the first person to get a predetermined number of points.

CARD GAMES

Before you even start playing card games, give your child the opportunity to explore the cards and become acquainted with them. A good way to do this is to suggest the following sorting activities:

- Place the black cards in one pile and the red ones in another.

- Find pairs of cards with matching numbers.

- Place all the cards of one suit together in a pile.

- Order the cards from one to ten, counting the ace as one and omitting the face cards.

When you do play games, don't hesitate to simplify the rules. You can work up to a more challenging version when your child is ready.

For all the games described here, remove the jokers.

Making a Card Holder

It is difficult for young children to hold and use more than three or four cards at a time. You can make a card holder using two plastic lids from margarine tubs or coffee cans. Punch a hole in the center of each lid and place the lids back to back. Push a brad through the holes and bend it back to fasten the lids together. (Brads can be bought at stationery stores.) The cards can be held between the two lids.

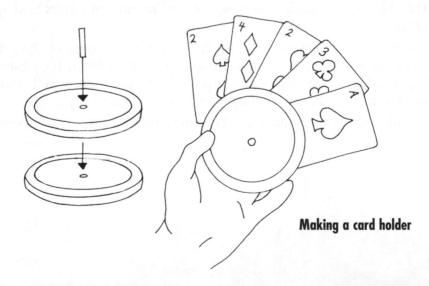

Making a card holder

Snap

Two to four people can play.

Deal the cards one at a time until there are no cards left. Players place their cards in a pile facedown in front of them.

Players turn over the top cards in their piles and place them faceup next to their piles. They continue in this way until two cards with the same number appear. The first person to call "Snap!" takes the two piles of faceup cards under the matching cards and puts them at the bottom of his facedown pile.

If two or more people call out "Snap!" at the same time, the piles with the matching cards are placed faceup in the center and called Snap Pool. When a card that matches the snap pool card appears, the first player to call out "Snap Pool!" adds the snap pool cards to her facedown pile.

A player is out of the game when he has no more cards. The winner is the person with all or most of the cards.

Go Fish

This game is for two or more players.

Deal five cards facedown to each player. Place the rest of the cards facedown in the center.

Players pick up their cards and arrange them in their hands by value—aces with aces, and so on. The object is to try to get four cards of the same value.

The first player asks any other player for a card that will help her complete a set of four cards. If the other player has the requested card he must give the card to the first player, who can then ask another player for another card.

If the other player does not have the requested card, he says "Go Fish." The first player picks up a card from the center pile, and her turn is over. When a player has four cards of equal value, these cards are placed facedown next to that player.

The winner is the first person to get rid of all cards in his or her hand. If two players finish together, the one with the most groups of four cards is the winner.

Variation: A simpler version of the game is to collect two instead of four cards of equal value.

War

This is a game for two players.

Deal the cards one at a time until all the cards have been dealt.

Players place their cards in a pile facedown in front of them. Both players turn over the top card on their piles. The player with the higher number wins both cards and adds them to the bottom of his or her pile. The king is the highest value, followed by the queen and then the jack. The ace counts as one.

If the two cards are the same, the players put down two more cards. The player with the higher card wins all four cards. Whoever collects all the cards wins.

Variation: Persian Pasha

Both players turn over the top cards in their piles and place them faceup in front of their piles. They continue to do so until both players turn up a card of the same suit. The player who has the higher card wins the cards in the opponent's faceup pile. In this game, the ace is the highest card.

Keep playing until one of the players wins all the cards or until two cards of the same suit cannot be turned up. The player with the most cards wins.

In War and Persian Pasha, it sometimes takes a while for one player to win all the cards. You can decide instead to play for a specified amount of time. Whoever has the most cards at the end of the time period wins.

Concentration

Two or more people can play Concentration.

The object of the game is to find pairs of matching cards among an array of facedown cards. Use a small number of pairs of cards to start with—say, six pairs—and slowly increase the number when your child seems ready for more.

Shuffle the cards and lay them out in rows and columns. The first player turns over two cards. If they are of equal value (e.g., two fours), the player keeps the two cards and takes another turn. If the two cards are different, the cards must be placed back in their same positions facedown. The next player takes a turn trying to find two matching cards.

As the game progresses, players must concentrate and try to remember where the different numbered cards are located. This will help when it is their turn again to try and pick two matching cards.

When all the cards have been collected, the person with the most cards wins.

Concentration

Pyramid

The explanation for Pyramid is more formidable than the game itself. It is a good game for you and your child to play together. One person can also play this game alone.

Remove the face cards. Shuffle the rest of the cards and lay 15 of them faceup in a pyramid formation. Keep the remaining undealt cards in a pile facedown in front of you.

The object of the game is to remove as many cards as possible from the pyramid, subject to these conditions:

- You can only remove cards from the pyramid that are not covered by any other card in the pyramid.

- You can only remove a pair of cards that add up to ten or one card with a value of ten.

- In this game, the ace has a value of one.

At the start of the game, only the bottom row of five cards is considered uncovered. The shorter upper rows are covered by the longer rows below. To begin play, check to see whether any two uncovered cards in the pyramid (i.e., the bottom row) add up to ten. If there is such a pair, take both cards and place them facedown in a tens pile. If there is a ten in the bottom row, place this card also in the tens pile.

Begin this game by taking the ace of clubs, the nine of spades, and the ten of clubs. Place them in the tens pile.

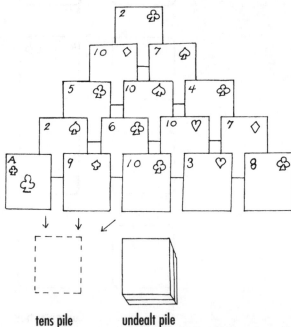

tens pile   undealt pile

Next, turn over the top card of the undealt pile. If this card is a ten, place it face down in the tens pile. If not, then check to see whether this card and any of the uncovered cards will add up to ten. If they do, take both cards and place them facedown in the tens pile. If you cannot use the top card, place it face-up in a pile called the discard pile.

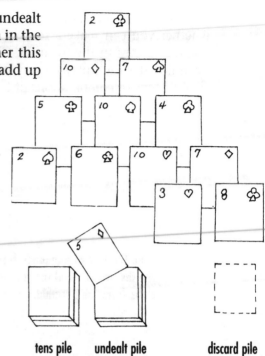

Place the five of diamonds from the undealt pile in the discard pile. Place the two of spades and the eight of clubs from the pyramid in the tens pile.

tens pile   undealt pile   discard pile

Keep turning over the top card from the undealt pile, checking to see whether it is a ten or adds up to ten with one of the uncovered cards in the pyramid.

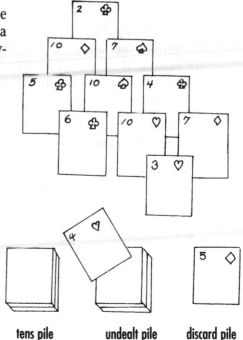

Take the six of clubs from the pyramid and the four of hearts from the undealt pile.

tens pile   undealt pile   discard pile

If you cannot make a ten with the top card of the undealt pile, look to see whether you can make a ten with the top card in the discard pile and an uncovered card in the pyramid. Check the pyramid after each play for any newly uncovered tens or combinations of ten.

Take the five of diamonds from the discard pile and the five of clubs from the pyramid.

tens pile   undealt pile   discard pile

When you have gone through all the cards in the undealt pile, go through the cards in the discard pile once again. The game is over when you have gone through the discard pile or removed all the cards in the pyramid, whichever comes first.

Variation: You can make the game easier for your child by writing out as a reference the number combinations that add up to ten.

Variation: This game can be made more difficult by including the face cards. You would then deal 28 cards in seven rows in the pyramid, and you would look for sums of 13 instead of 10. (The jack has a value of 11; the queen, 12; and the king, 13.)

COUNTING GAMES

Odds or Evens

Two or more people can play this game.

Each person receives the same number of beans, pennies, or pebbles. Ten or twelve is a good number to use.

Without letting anyone see, the first player picks up some of her pennies and asks the second player, "Odds or evens?" The second player has to guess whether there is an even or odd number of pennies in the first player's hand. If the guess is correct, the first player gives the second player two of her pennies. If the guess is incorrect, the second player gives the first player two pennies.

The second player then picks up some of his pennies and asks the third player, "Odds or evens?"

If there are two players, continue playing until one person wins all the pennies. If there are more than two players, the game should be timed. After 5 minutes (or whatever time period is chosen), the person with the most pennies wins.

Children will be interested to know that the number 0 is even.

Pennies in a Circle

Two or more people can play this game.

Arrange any number of pennies and one quarter in a circle. The quarter is called the king.

Starting from any penny in the circle, each player takes a turn, counting and touching each coin as it is counted. If the coin that is touched at the count of ten is a penny, remove it from the circle.

If a player lands on the king at the count of ten, that player is out. Do not remove the king from the circle.

The last player left is the winner. If all the pennies are gone and only the king remains, then all the players left are winners.

Variation: Count to a number other than 10.

GAMES WITH DICE

Beetle

You can play this game with two to four players. Only one die is needed.

The object of the game is to be the first person to finish drawing a beetle.

Each person takes a turn rolling the die. Each number on the die represents one part of the beetle's body. The body parts must be drawn in the order specified, as follows:

When you roll a 1 or a 6, you can draw the body. You cannot start adding any other parts until you have drawn the body.

Once the body is drawn, you need to throw a 2 for the head or a 3 for a leg. You can draw the head and the legs in any order. You need to roll six 3's, not necessarily in consecutive order, to complete the legs.

Once you have drawn the head, you can draw the eyes or the feelers while waiting for all the 3's for the legs. You need to roll a 5 for each eye and a 4 for each feeler, not necessarily in consecutive order. The first player to finish the drawing wins.

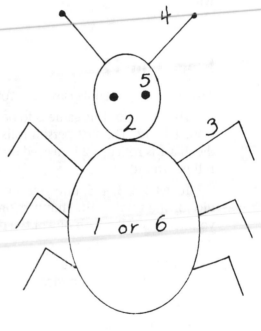

Beetle

Going to Boston

Two or more people can play this game. You need three dice.

The first person throws the three dice and sets the die with the highest number aside with the rolled number up. If the highest number is on two of the dice, remove either die.

Now, roll the remaining two dice and again set aside the die with the higher number.

Roll the third die. Add up the total on the three dice. (Players can use a calculator to do the adding.) This is the player's score for this round.

After a specified number of rounds, the person with the highest total score wins.

From 1 to 12

Any number of people can play. You need two dice.

The object of this game is to be the first person to throw the dice in order from 1 to 12. The first person rolls both dice and hopes to get a 1 on either die. If a 1 is rolled, a 2 is needed on the next round. Each player only gets one roll per round.

To get a 2, 3, 4, 5, or 6 you can use either the number on only one of the dice or the total of the numbers on both dice. For example, if you need a 5, you need to roll a 5 on one of the dice, or a 1 and a 4, or a 2 and a 3 on both dice.

For the remaining numbers, 7 through 12, you will need to use the total of the numbers on both dice.

Variation: To simplify the game, the winner can be the first person to get to 6 or any agreed-upon number.

GUESSING GAMES

Guess the Number

Two or more people can play this game.

The object of the game is to try to guess the number that one of the players is thinking of.

Before starting, players must choose the range of numbers (e.g., between 1 and 10, 1 and 20, or 1 and 100).

To play, the first player secretly chooses a number and the other players take turns guessing. The first player indicates whether the guess is too high or too low. Play continues until the correct number is guessed.

Then the roles are switched and another player thinks of a number.

How Many?

This is a game for two or more players.

Each player is given the same number of beans; 15 or 20 is fine.

The first player secretly places from zero to five beans in her hand. Then, showing the closed fist, she asks the second player, "How many?" If the second player guesses correctly, that player gets all the held beans. If the first player is holding zero beans and the second player guesses correctly, the first player gives the second player two beans. If the second player's guess is wrong, he has to give the first player two beans.

The second player then hides some of his beans and asks the third player, "How many?"

The person who gets all the beans is the winner. Or after a certain agreed-upon time period, the person with the most beans wins.

GAMES WITH SHAPES

Squares

Two or more people can play this game.

The object of the game is to connect the dots, one line at a time, to make squares.

First, draw a grid of dots. The grid can be as small or as large as you like.

The first player draws a line to join two dots. The next player does the same thing.

As the grid gets filled in with lines, players are able to complete a square and write their initials in it. Each time a square is completed, that player is allowed to draw another line joining two dots. Sometimes players can complete a few squares on one turn. When all the squares are completed, players count the number of squares that have their initials in them. The player with the most completed squares wins.

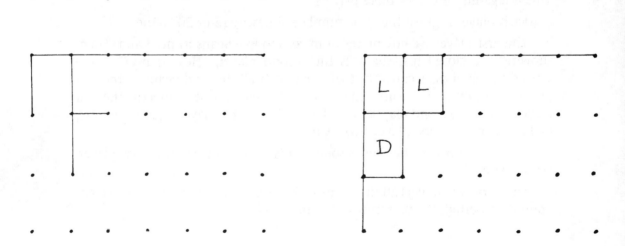

Squares

Three in a Row

Two people play this game.

First, draw a 49-square grid. Players then choose their symbols, such as their initials. The aim is for players to get three of their symbols in a row as many times as they can, while preventing their opponent from doing the same.

Players take turns adding one symbol at a time to the grid. Rows can be made horizontally, vertically, or diagonally. When a row of three is completed, the player draws a line through the three symbols. Players keep a tally of how many groups of three they have made. The winner is the player with the highest tally after all the squares are filled.

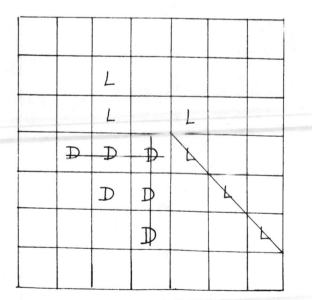
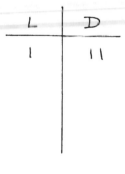

Three in a Row

Tangrams

This is an ideal game for one child to play alone.

The tangram is an ancient Chinese design that is made up of a square divided into seven shapes: five triangles, one square, and one parallelogram. Many different figures and patterns can be made from these seven pieces. Although all seven are supposed to be used in completing a design, your child can use only a few of the shapes if desired.

You can make your own tangram by photocopying the one on this page. Glue the photocopy to a piece of white poster board. Both sides of the tangram pieces should be the same color. Cut the pieces apart, then let your child try putting them together in different shapes.

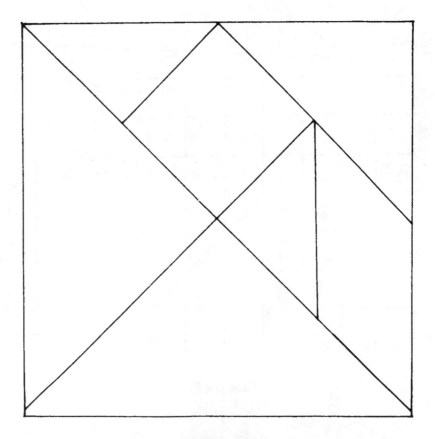

Tangram pattern

Your child can copy these tangram shapes to get a feel for the game. Encourage your child to make other designs that can be abstract or represent particular objects.

Tangram shapes

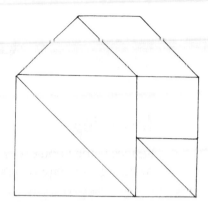

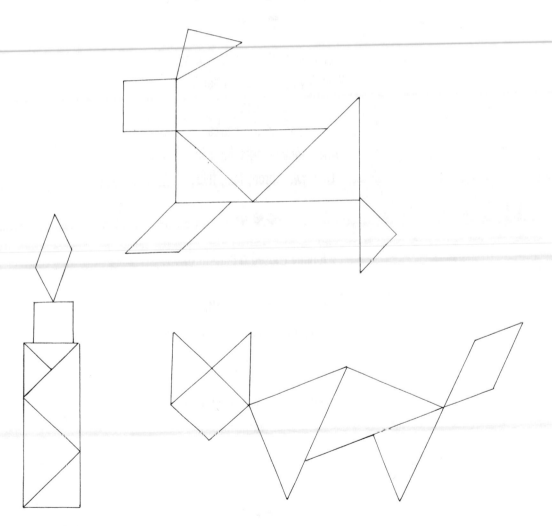

OUTDOOR GAMES

Jump Rope

Besides being good exercise, jumping rope provides excellent opportunities for counting. Here are two popular counting chants.

Cinderella, dressed in yellow,
Went downstairs to kiss her fellow.
By mistake
She kissed a snake.
How many doctors did it take?
One, two, three, four, five…

Johnny chased a blackbird.
Johnny chased a bee.
Johnny broke a bottle
And blamed it on me.
I told Ma
And Ma told Pa,
And Johnny got a whipping,
Wah wah wah.
How many whippings did Johnny get?
One, two, three, four, five…

Hopscotch

There are many versions of this game, which goes by many different names. Here is a favorite one.

Draw the hopscotch pattern on the sidewalk with chalk.

The traditional marker to use is a stone. However, younger players will find a beanbag easier to throw.

To begin, player A throws the marker so that it lands in square 1. Player A hops over square 1 to square 2 landing on one foot. Player A then continues hopping toward sky blue, landing on one foot in squares 3, 6, and 9, and on both feet simultaneously in squares 4 and 5, 7 and 8, and sky blue.

On reaching sky blue, player A jumps to turn around, then hops back again the same way, stopping on one foot at square 2 to bend over and pick up the marker in square 1. After picking up the marker, the player may hop in that square.

Player B does the same. On the next turn, player A throws the marker in square 2 and repeats the hops and jumps, this time jumping over square 2. The object of the game is to get to sky blue, by throwing the marker in each square consecutively.

Older players pay attention to such matters as throwing accurately inside the lines, not stepping on lines, and not falling off balance. Younger players need to be given a lot of latitude or they will get frustrated. For example, it may be easier to land in all squares on both feet.

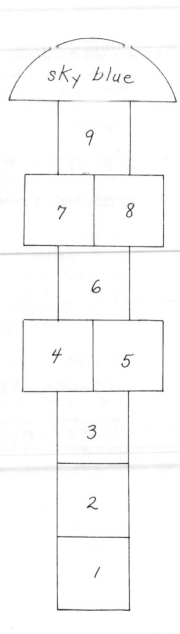

Hopscotch pattern

Aiming for the Target

This game has a number of versions. Here are three. Pebbles or beans can be used, and two or more people can play.

VERSION 1

Two players stand about 20 feet (6 m) away from a hole in the ground. Choose a distance that is challenging but not too far for your child to throw successfully. The size of the hole depends on the age and dexterity of the child. If you cannot find a satisfactory hole, use a bucket, a bowl, or any container. Each player gets one pebble. Players take turns trying to throw their pebbles into the hole.

If the pebble lands in the hole, the player gets four points. If nobody's pebble falls into the hole, the player whose pebble is closer to the hole gets a point. If the second player's pebble hits that of the first player, no points are scored. The winner is the player with the most points at the end of five rounds, or the first person to get 20 points.

VERSION 2

For this game, each player gets 10 beans or pebbles and throws them one at a time into the hole. After throwing all the pebbles, the player picks up and keeps the pebbles that landed in the hole. The other pebbles are left on the ground. The next player takes a turn, also keeping the pebbles that went into the hole.

On the second round, players collect and share the pebbles from the ground. If the pebbles cannot be shared equally, the extra pebbles are left on the ground. Players again take turns aiming for the hole and keeping the ones that land in the hole. After two or three rounds, the player with the most pebbles wins.

VERSION 3

The target in this game can be any design agreed upon by the players. The target is drawn in chalk on the sidewalk.

Each player gets one pebble. Players take turns throwing their pebbles from a designated starting line. (Younger children will find it easier to use beanbags.)

If the pebble or beanbag falls within the target, the player gets the number of points written in that zone of the target. If the pebble or beanbag falls on a line between zones, the player gets the points of the zone with the lower value. Scores are recorded. When all the players have had a turn, the next round begins. After an agreed-upon number of rounds, the player with the highest score wins.

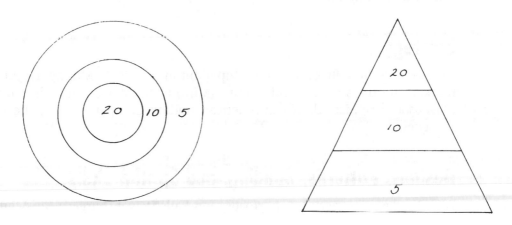

Target patterns

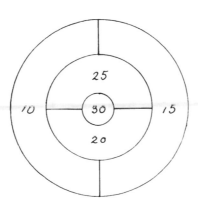

COMMERCIAL GAMES

Many commercial games provide mathematical experiences for children. The following list of games includes those that we have used in our classrooms and others that have been recommended to us by our colleagues. They are listed according to the skills and concepts they cover.

Counting

Hi-Ho! Cherry-O (Western Publishing); Sorry (Parker Brothers); Candy Land (Milton Bradley); Chutes and Ladders (Milton Bradley); Shut the Box (Great American Trading Company).

Strategy

Parcheesi (Milton Bradley); Battleship (Milton Bradley); Monopoly Junior (Parker Brothers); Connect Four (Milton Bradley); Up the River (Ravensburger); Mancala (Great American Trading Company). Also, checkers and chess.

Designs, Patterns, Building, and Spatial Skills

Differix (Ravensburger); Rivers, Roads, and Rails (Ravensburger); Mr. Mighty Mind (Leisure Living); Mr. Super Mind (Leisure Living); Brainy Blocks (Orda Ind Ltd.); Crystal Creations (Small World Toys); Tangoes (Rex Games). Also wooden building blocks, puzzles, mazes, tangrams, and marble runs.

Chapter 8

Counting Rhymes and Stories

There are many children's books that convey mathematical concepts. Some are specifically written to explain a mathematical idea; others just happen to have a mathematical aspect. Children's literature taps into the world of fantasy, humor, and the interests of young people. It is a wonderful resource for showing children that numbers and mathematics are everywhere. Reading these books with children gives them the opportunity to express mathematical ideas and enhances and develops their understanding of number.

This chapter contains a few poems and stories that focus on counting. Counting is part of a child's earliest introduction to mathematics and forms the basis for an understanding of our number system.

Meaningful counting includes several different components:

1. Knowing the correct sequence of the numbers.

2. Knowing that when a collection of objects is counted, each object is counted only once.

3. Knowing that the number given to the last object counted represents the total number of objects.

These are not easy concepts for children, and they need numerous opportunities to practice.

When you read these poems and stories with your child, you may sometimes wish to stop and ask questions that focus on the mathematics. It is also fine simply to respond to your child's spontaneous reaction to the material. It is important that you both enjoy and look forward to the experience and that your child feels comfortable expressing ideas and asking questions.

ROTE COUNTING

Children enjoy the rhythm of rote counting, and rhymes help them learn the correct sequence of numbers. Most rhymes do not go beyond 10 or 20, but a good understanding of the number sequence from 1 to 10 lays the foundation for the numbers that come afterward.

One, two, three, four,
Mary at the cottage door,
Five, six, seven, eight,
Eating cherries off a plate.

♦

One for the money,
Two for the show,
Three to make ready,
And four to go.

♦

One, two, three,
I love coffee,
And Billy loves tea,
How good you be,
One, two, three,
I love coffee,
And Billy loves tea.

1, 2, 3, 4, 5, 6, 7;

All good children go to heaven.

1, 2, 3, 4, 5, 6, 7, 8;

All bad children have to wait.

1 penny in the water

2 pennies on the sea

3 pennies on the railway

1, 2, 3.

Oliver-Oliver-Oliver Twist
Bet you a penny you can't do this:
Number one—touch your tongue
Number two—touch your shoe
Number three—touch your knee
Number four—touch the floor
Number five—stay alive
Number six—wiggle your hips
Number seven—jump to Heaven
Number eight—bang the gate
Number nine—walk the line
Number ten—start again.

One, two, three, four, five,
Once I caught a fish alive,

Six, seven, eight, nine, ten,
Then I let it go again.

Why did you let it go?
Because it bit my finger so.

Which finger did it bite?
The little finger on the right.

1, 2, 3, 4,
Preacher's at the chapel door.
5, 6, 7, 8,
Wonder who will come in late.
In comes Cat, in comes Rat,
In comes the lady with the
great big hat.

One for sorrow, two for joy,
Three for a girl, four for a boy,
Five for silver, six for gold,
Seven for a secret ne'er to be told.

One potato	Four potato	Six potato	Eight potato
Two potato	Five potato	Seven potato	Nine potato
Three potato	Six potato	Eight potato	Ten potato
FOUR	MORE	SHOUT	OUT

1, 2,
Buckle my shoe;

3, 4,
Shut the door;

5, 6,
Pick up sticks;

7, 8,
Lay them straight;

9, 10,
A big fat hen;

11, 12,
Dig and delve;

13, 14,
Maids are courting;

15, 16,
Maids in the kitchen;

17, 18,
Maids are waiting;

19, 20,
My plate is empty.

Mingle-dee, pingle-dee
Clap-clap-clap.
How many fingers do I
hold in my lap?

Would you say one?
Would you say two?
Raspberries, strawberries,
Fresh with dew.

Would you say three?
Would you say four?
Rutabaga, pumpkins,
Onion and corn.

Would you say five?
Would you say six?
Dandelions, crocuses,
Hickory sticks.

Would you say seven?
Would you say eight?
Eggs and cheese muffins.
On a dinner plate.

Would you say nine?
Would you say ten?
Then open your eyes,
And count them again.

Mingle-dee, pingle-dee
Clap-clap-clap.
How many fingers do I
hold in my lap?

One, I see,
  Two, I see,
    Three, I see,
      Four, I see,
        Five, I see,
          Six, I see,
            Seven, I see,
              Eight, I see,
                Nine, I see—TENNESSEE!

THE ANTS GO MARCHING

The ants go marching 1 by 1
Hurrah! Hurrah!
The ants go marching 1 by 1
Hurrah! Hurrah!
The ants go marching 1 by 1
And the little one stops to have some fun,
And they all go marching
Down and around
And into the ground
To get out of the rain.

The ants go marching 2 by 2,
And the little one stops to tie his shoe…

The ants go marching 3 by 3,
And the little one stops to climb a tree…

The ants go marching 4 by 4,
And the little one stops to shut
the door…

The ants go marching 5 by 5,
And the little one stops to take a dive…

The ants go marching 6 by 6,
And the little one stops to pick up
sticks…

The ants go marching 7 by 7,
And the little one stops to go to
heaven…

The ants go marching 8 by 8,
And the little one stops to shut the
gate…

The ants go marching 9 by 9,
And the little one stops to pick up a
dime…

The ants go marching 10 by 10
And the little one stops and shouts,
"The End!"

THIS OLD MAN

This old man, he played one,

He played nick-nack on my thumb,

With a nick-nack patty-wack, give your dog a bone,

This old man came rolling home.

This old man, he played two,

He played nick-nack on my shoe,

With a nick-nack patty-wack, give your dog a bone,

This old man came rolling home.

This old man, he played three,...on my knee,...

This old man, he played four,...at my door,...

This old man, he played five,...on his tie,...

This old man, he played six,...on some sticks,...

This old man, he played seven,...up to heaven,...

This old man, he played eight,...at my gate,...

This old man, he played nine,...on a dime,...

This old man, he played ten, once again....

COUNTING BACKWARD

Counting backward is an important skill that helps lay the foundation for subtraction. It is also another way to help children become familiar with the number system.

There are many poems that involve counting backward. Most start with the numbers 5 or 10.

FIVE LITTLE MONKEYS

Five little monkeys walked along

the shore;

One went a-sailing,

Then there were four.

Four little monkeys climbed up a tree;

One of them tumbled down,

Then there were three.

Three little monkeys found a pot of glue;

One got stuck in it,

Then there were two.

Two little monkeys found a currant bun;

One ran away with it,

Then there was one.

One little monkey cried all afternoon,

So they put him in an aeroplane

And sent him to the moon.

TEN LITTLE GRASSHOPPERS

Ten little grasshoppers sitting on a vine;
One ate too much corn, and then there were nine.

Nine little grasshoppers swinging on a gate;
One fell off, and then there were eight.

Eight little grasshoppers started off to Devon;
One lost his way, then there were seven.

Seven little grasshoppers lived between two bricks;
Along came a windstorm, then there were six.

Six little grasshoppers found a beehive;
One found a bumblebee, then there were five.

Five little grasshoppers playing on the floor;
Pussycat passed that way, then there were four.

Four little grasshoppers playing near a tree;
One chased a buzzy fly, then there were three.

Three little grasshoppers looked for pastures new;
A turkey gobbler saw them, then there were two.

Two little grasshoppers sitting in the sun;
A little boy went fishing, then there was one.

One little grasshopper left all alone;
He tried to find his brothers, then there were none.

When your child is ready to count down from numbers higher than 10, you can improvise with some of the rhymes you know. With these poems, you can start and end with any number. So you could start with 22 frogs and continue until you have 7 frogs left, or with 51 leaves and continue until you have 40 left.

Five Little Frogs

Five little frogs sitting on a well,
One looked in and down he fell.
Frogs jump high,
Frogs jump low.
Four little frogs dancing to and fro.

Four little frogs sitting on a well, etc.

Five Little Leaves

Five little leaves so bright and gay
Were dancing about a tree one sunny day.
The wind came blowing through the town,
One little leaf came falling down.

Four little leaves so bright and gay, etc.

SKIP COUNTING— FORWARD AND BACKWARD

This Liberian folktale illustrates the idea that skip counting—counting by twos, threes, fives, tens, and so on—is sometimes a less time-consuming and more efficient way to count. This is especially true when numbers are large. Skip counting introduces children to the ideas of adding, subtracting, and multiplying.

ANOTHER WAY TO COUNT TO TEN

In the jungle, behind an old vine tree that shaded a mighty stream, a great leopard named Pallo ruled the animal kingdom.

One day Pallo's daughter, Sayla, found her father resting alone. "Father," she said, "why do you sit here looking so sad? The Festival of Twenty Drums has started and all of the animals are asking for you." Not far away, Pallo could hear the beating of the drums. "One, two, three, four. One, two, three, four. Thump, bump, thump, bump."

"Sayla, I am worried. I am getting older and I wonder who will help you rule when I no longer can. You will be a wise and caring ruler, but who will be your prince?"

All of a sudden, Pallo jumped to his feet. "I have a wonderful idea!" he said. "We shall choose the new prince at the festival! He must be the wisest of all in the land."

"Father," Sayla asked, "how will we discover who is the smartest of all?"

"You shall see, my daughter," said Pallo.

When Pallo and Sayla arrived at the festival, everyone was celebrating and dancing to the twenty drums. The drum players filled the jungle with wonderful rhythms. "One, two, three, four. One, two, three, four. Thump, bump. Thump, bump." Pallo commanded the drummers to stop drumming and the dancers to stop dancing.

Pallo jumped on top of a large tree stump and said, "Listen to me, my friends. Today we will choose a prince for Princess Sayla who will marry her and help her rule this jungle in peace. The one who is chosen must be the wisest of all."

The animals were very excited and started chattering to each other. It would be the greatest honor to be chosen as the next ruler of the kingdom.

King Pallo held his hunting spear high in the air. "Look at this, everyone." He threw the spear up into the sky, so high that the animals could see it touch the highest leaves of the tallest tree. As it landed on the ground in front of him, he said, "Each animal who wants to become Prince must step up and throw it so high that he can count to ten before it drops to the earth again."

The animals thought this was going to be easy. King Pallo ordered the drummers to signal the beginning of the contest. The animals formed a circle so they could watch and cheer. The first one to try was the big, gray elephant. He lumbered past the other animals. He grabbed the spear, threw it into the air, and began to count, "One, two, three," but then the spear came down out of the sky and landed in front of him. He had counted very slowly. He was disappointed that he had not won and walked away with his big trunk hanging down to the ground.

Next to try was the powerful lion. He stepped into the circle of animals and shook his red-yellow mane. He roared and said, "King Pallo, I will send this spear up to the sun and when I do, I will become the great ruler of this kingdom." He looked up to the sun and with all his might flung the spear above him and began counting in his loud voice, "One, two, three, four, five," but before he could say "six," the spear pierced the ground in front of him. He was very embarrassed.

The chimpanzee was eager for his turn. Holding a vine, he swung into the circle. He sang a song very fast to show everyone that he would soon win. All the animals watched his long arm throw the spear above him, while he shouted, "One, two, three, four, five, six, seven." Everyone thought that he would surely get to ten, but before he did the spear flew down and hit the ground. Even with his fast talking, he couldn't win. Everyone became silent because surely if the quick chimpanzee could not win, no one could. The King and Sayla looked sad. King Pallo said, "It seems that no one is clever enough to win this challenge."

Suddenly, a young antelope stepped into the circle and quietly said, "Please, let me try. I will be a good husband to Sayla and a wise ruler of this kingdom."

The King and all of the animals looked at each other in surprise. The antelope was graceful but did not look very strong. If the elephant, the great lion, and the quick chimpanzee could not win, how could the antelope? They thought it was silly for him to try, but King Pallo said, "I promised that anyone who wanted to could try to meet my challenge."

The antelope smiled at Sayla. He had been her good friend for many years, and she secretly hoped he would win. The antelope stepped to the spear and skillfully threw the spear upward. Before it could fall down to the earth, he said simply, "Five, ten!" The spear fell down. "I have done it," he said. "The king did not tell me how to count to ten. I counted by fives and I have won!"

The animals were amazed. King Pallo walked over to the antelope and said, "The antelope has proven that he is the one clever enough to be the next ruler, for after all, he has shown us another way to count to ten!"

—Retold by Rachel Kohrman

If you want to count the way the antelope did, go, "Five, ten, fifteen, twenty…"

There are very few poems that focus on skip counting. However, you can be creative with poems that you know.

One Elephant

1 elephant went out to play
Upon a spider's web one day.
He found it such enormous fun
That he called for another elephant to come.

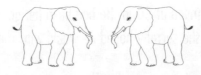

Children love to add their own verses, and instead of calling for one elephant to come, you can call two elephants at a time.

1 elephant went out to play
Upon a spider's web one day.
He found it such enormous fun
That he called for 2 more elephants to come.

3 elephants went out to play
Upon a spider's web one day.
They found it such enormous fun
That they called for 2 more elephants to come.

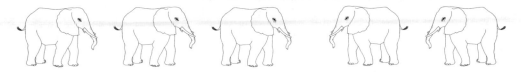

You can vary the poem and start and increase by any number of elephants.

You can do the same with "Ten Fat Sausages," starting with any number of sausages in the pan.

10 fat sausages sitting in the pan;
One went "POP!" and another went "BANG!"

8 fat sausages sitting in the pan;
One went "POP!" and another went "BANG!"

6 fat sausages sitting in the pan;
One went "POP!" and another went "BANG!"

4 fat sausages sitting in the pan;
One went "POP!" and another went "BANG!"

2 fat sausages sitting in the pan;
One went "POP!" and another went "BANG!"

0 fat sausages sitting in the pan.

MEANINGFUL COUNTING

For children to understand that when they count objects, they cannot miss any or count any more than once, they need a lot of experience actually counting objects of all shapes and sizes.

Children love counting the number of animals the lady swallowed.

There was an old lady who swallowed a fly.
I don't know why she swallowed a fly.
Perhaps she'll die.

There was an old lady who swallowed a spider.
That wiggled and tiggled and jiggled inside her.
She swallowed the spider to catch the fly.
I don't know why she swallowed a fly.
Perhaps she'll die.

There was an old lady who swallowed a bird.
How absurd! She swallowed a bird.
She swallowed the bird to catch the spider.
That wiggled and tiggled and jiggled inside her.
She swallowed the spider to catch the fly,
I don't know why she swallowed a fly.
Perhaps she'll die.

There was an old lady who swallowed a cat.
Think of that! She swallowed a cat.
She swallowed the cat to catch the bird.
She swallowed the bird to catch the spider.
That wiggled and tiggled and jiggled inside her.
She swallowed the spider to catch the fly,
I don't know why she swallowed a fly.
Perhaps she'll die.

There was an old lady who swallowed a dog.

What a hog! She swallowed a dog.

She swallowed the dog to catch the cat,

She swallowed the cat to catch the bird,

She swallowed the bird to catch the spider.

That wiggled and tiggled and jiggled inside her.

She swallowed the spider to catch the fly,

I don't know why she swallowed a fly.

Perhaps she'll die.

There was an old lady who swallowed a cow.

I don't know how she swallowed the cow.

She swallowed the cow to catch the dog,

She swallowed the dog to catch the cat,

She swallowed the cat to catch the bird,

She swallowed the bird to catch the spider.

That wiggled and tiggled and jiggled inside her.

She swallowed the spider to catch the fly,

I don't know why she swallowed a fly.

Perhaps she'll die.

There was an old lady who swallowed a horse.

She's dead, of course.

"The Seven Silly Fishermen" is a folktale found in different forms in many cultures. Help your child discover the mistake each silly fisherman makes when he counts.

THE SEVEN SILLY FISHERMEN

Once upon a time, seven fishermen decided to go fishing. They came to the bank of a stream and spread out along it, each casting his line into the water to catch fish.

At the end of the day, they all gathered together and prepared to go home. "Just a minute," said one. "We'd better make sure we're all here!"

"I know what to do," said another. "Let's count and see."

The first fisherman began to count. He pointed to the other fishermen and said, "One, two, three, four, five, six! Oh no! One of us is missing!"

"Just a minute," said another. "Let me count." He began again, pointing to each of the other fishermen, saying, "One, two, three, four, five, six! Only six! One of us must have drowned."

Each of the fishermen counted, but each time they could only count to six.

"What shall we do?" they cried.

Just then, along came a little boy.

"Why are you all standing about crying? What is your trouble?"

"Oh," cried the silly fishermen all together. "We are crying because seven of us came out to fish, and now there are only six of us. One of us must have drowned!"

The little boy looked at them and said, "If I can find your missing friend, will you give me half the fish in your baskets? I have not eaten since early morning.

"Yes! Yes!" cried the fishermen. "Only find our friend, and you can have as many fish as you want."

"Very well," said the little boy, "Now, watch!" He pointed at each silly fisherman and began to count as he pointed. "One, two, three, four, five, six, seven. Seven silly fishermen came out to fish, and seven of you will go back."

"Oh, thank you!" cried the fishermen. "You found the missing one of us!"

—Retold by Dorothy Freedman

As children's sense of number develops, they are able to answer "how many?" without actually counting. If they are given five candies, they can tell that they have five without counting each candy. An exact answer is possible if the quantity is small enough. When the quantity increases, estimates are in order.

These poems deal with small, easily recognized quantities.

Twos

Why are lots of things in two?
Hands on clocks, and gloves and shoes.

Scissor-blades, and water taps,
Collar studs, and luggage straps.

Walnut shells and pigeons' eggs.
Arms and eyes and ears and legs

Will you kindly tell me who's
So fond of making things in twos?

—John Drinkwater

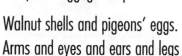

Five Fingers

Five fingers on this hand,
Five fingers on that;
A dear little nose,
A mouth like a rose,
Two cheeks so tiny and fat.
Two eyes, two ears,
And ten little toes;
That's the way the baby grows.

COUNTING ON

Like skip counting, counting on is a more sophisticated way to count.

THE POSTMAN

Eight o'clock,
The postman's knock!
5 letters for Papa;

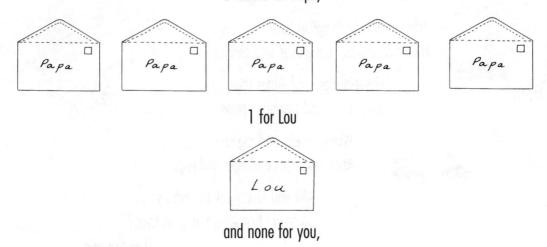

1 for Lou

and none for you,

And 3 for dear Mamma.

—Christina G. Rossetti

How many letters? You can count each one, or you can start with five and count on from there.

These poems also offer many counting opportunities.

TWO MOTHER PIGS

Two mother pigs lived in a pen,

Each had four babies, and that made ten.

These four babies were black as night,

These four babies were black and white.

But all eight babies loved to play

And they rolled and rolled in the mud all day.

At night, with their mother, they curled up in a heap,

And squealed and squealed till they went to sleep.

POTATOES IN A POT

3 potatoes in a pot,
Take 2 out and leave 1 hot.
1 for me, 2 for you,
And here's the hot potato, too!

For a challenge you can change the number of potatoes in the pot.

THREE LITTLE RATS

Three little rats with black felt hats,

Three little ducks with cricket bats,

Three little dogs with curling tails,

Three little cats with bright red pails,

Went out to play with two little pigs,
In satin vests and curly wigs.

But suddenly it chanced to rain,
And so they all went home again.

With many of the poems, you can read them as they are, or for a challenge, change the numbers.

Cluck-Cluck-Cluck

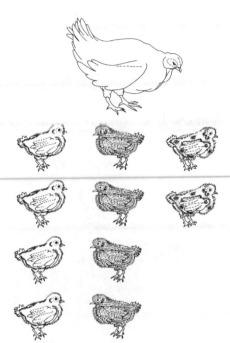

Cluck, cluck, cluck,
Good morning, Mrs. Hen.
How many chickens have you got?
Madam, I've got 10.
4 of them are yellow,
4 of them are brown,
2 of them are speckled,
The nicest in the town.
Cluck, cluck, cluck,
Cock-a-doodle-doo!

Cluck, cluck, cluck,
Good morning, Mrs. Hen
How many chickens have you got?
Madam, I've got 10.
5 of them are yellow,
2 of them are brown,
3 of them are speckled,
The nicest in the town.
Cluck, cluck, cluck,
Cock-a-doodle-doo!

TEN GALLOPING HORSES

10 galloping horses came to town,
5 were white and 5 were brown,
They galloped up, they galloped down,
And then they galloped right out of town.

You can have seven white horses and three brown ones or whatever combination you and your child decide.

THERE WAS A KING

There was a king who had four sons,
For breakfast they had currant buns,
It seems a funny thing to me,
But every day they each ate three.
Every day the baker came,
Every day it was the same,
Every day at half past eight
He left twelve buns at the castle gate.

How would the poem change if each son decided to eat four buns instead of three?

Recommended Reading

If you have enjoyed the combination of reading and mathematics, the following is a list of books that we have used and others that are favorites of colleagues and other parents. If a book is available in paperback, we have included the date and publication of the paperback edition.

Thiessen, Dianne, and Margaret Matthias. *The Wonderful World of Mathematics*. Reston, VA. National Council of Teachers of Mathematics, 1992.

This gives an annotated bibliography of children's books that cover a variety of mathematical concepts.

Number

COUNTING RHYMES

Aylesworth, Jim. *One Crow: A Counting Rhyme*. New York: HarperCollins, 1990.

Eichenberg, Fritz. *Dancing in the Moon: Counting Rhymes*. New York: Harcourt Brace and Co., 1975.

Sullivan, Charles. *Numbers at Play: A Counting Book*. New York: Rizzoli International, 1992.

COUNTING BACKWARDS

Bang, Molly. *Ten, Nine, Eight*. New York: William Morrow and Co., 1991.

Ernst, Lisa. *Up to Ten and Down Again*. New York: Lothrop, Lee, and Shepard, 1986.

Gerstein, Mordecai. *Roll Over!* New York: Crown Books for Young Readers, 1984.

Rees, Mary. *Ten in a Bed*. Boston: Little, Brown, and Co., 1988.

Russo, Marisabina. *Only Six More Days*. New York: Greenwillow Books, 1988.

Sendak, Maurice. *One Was Johnny: A Counting Book*. New York: HarperCollins, 1991.

SKIP COUNTING

Demi. *Demi's Count the Animals 1-2-3*. New York: Putnam, 1990.

Hoban, Tana. *Count and See*. New York: Macmillan Children's Books, 1972.

Hong, Lily Toy. *Two of Everything*. Morton Grove, IL: Albert Whitman and Co., 1993.

MEANINGFUL COUNTING

Anno, Mitsumasa. *Anno's Counting Book*. New York: HarperCollins, 1986.

Blumenthal, Nancy. *Count-a-Saurus*. New York: Macmillan Children's Books, 1992.

Carle, Eric. *1,2,3 to the Zoo*. New York: Philomel Books, 1989.

_____. *Rooster's Off to See the World*. Natick, MA: Picture Book Studio, 1987.

_____. *The Very Hungry Caterpillar*. New York: Philomel Books, 1991.

Carter, David. *How Many Bugs in A Box?* New York: Simon and Schuster, 1988.

de Regniers, Beatrice Schenk. *So Many Cats!* New York: Houghton Mifflin, 1985.

Feelings, Muriel. *Moja Means One: A Swahili Counting Book*. New York: Dial Books for Young Readers, 1976.

Giganti, Paul. *How Many Snails? A Counting Book*. New York: Greenwillow Books, 1988.

Grossman, Virginia. *Ten Little Rabbits*. San Francisco: Chronicle Books, 1991.

Hamm, Diane J. *How Many Feet in the Bed?* New York: Simon and Schuster, 1991.

Harada, Joyce. *It's the 0, 1, 2, 3 Book*. Union City, CA: Heian International, 1985.

Hoban, Tana. *1,2,3*. New York: Greenwillow Books, 1985.

Hutchins, Pat. *One Hunter*. New York: Greenwillow Books, 1982.

McMillan, Bruce. *Counting Wildflowers*. New York: Lothrop, Lee, and Shepard, 1986.

Morozumi, Atsuko. *One Gorilla*. New York: Farrar, Straus, and Giroux, 1993.

Zaslavsky, Claudia. *Count on Your Fingers African Style*. New York: HarperCollins Children's Books, 1980.

COUNTING MORE THAN TWENTY

Estes, Eleanor. *The Hundred Dresses*. New York: Harcourt Brace and Co., 1974.

Gag, Wanda. *Millions of Cats*. New York: Putnam, 1977.

Hoban, Tana. *Count and See*. New York: Macmillan, 1972.

Howard, Katherine. *I Can Count to One Hundred...Can You?* New York: Random House, 1979.

Peppe, Rodney. *Circus Numbers*. New York: Delacorte, 1969.

Schwartz, David M. *How Much Is a Million?* New York: William Morrow, and Co., 1993.

EARLY ADDITION, SUBTRACTION, MULTIPLICATION, AND DIVISION

Anno, Mitsumasa. *Anno's Counting House*. New York: Philomel Books, 1982.

Brown, Marcia. *Stone Soup*. New York: Aladdin Books, 1986.

Burningham, John. *Mr. Gumpy's Outing*. New York: Henry Holt and Co., 1990.

Butler, M. Christina. *Too Many Eggs*. Boston: David R. Godine, 1988.

Hutchins, Pat. *The Doorbell Rang*. New York: William Morrow and Co., 1989.

Mathews, Louise. *Bunches and Bunches of Bunnies*. New York: Scholastic, 1991.

Pattern

Anno, Mitsumasa. *Anno's Math Games*. New York: Putnam, 1987.

Asch, Frank. *Moonbear's Books*. New York: Little Simon, 1993.

Baer, Gene. *THUMP, THUMP, Rat a Tat-Tat*. New York: HarperTrophy, 1991.

Eastman, P. D. *Go Dog Go*. New York: Random House, 1961.

Ernst, Bruno. *The Magic Mirror of M. C. Escher*. Jersey City, NJ: Parkwest Publications, 1991.

Carle, Eric. *Today Is Monday*. New York: Putnam, 1993.

Keats, Ezra Jack. *The Snowy Day*. New York: Puffin Books, 1976.

Lionni, Leo. *Fish Is Fish*. New York: Alfred A. Knopf, 1987.

McKissack, Patricia. *Flossie and the Fox*. New York: Deal Books, 1986.

Morris, Ann. *Bread, Bread, Bread*. New York: Mulberry, 1993.

Morris, Ann. *Hats, Hats, Hats*. New York: Mulberry, 1993.

Pinkney, Brian. *Max Found Two Sticks*. New York: Simon and Schuster, 1994.

Roy, Ron. *Whose Shoes Are These?* New York: Clarion Books, 1988.

Schattschneider, D. *Visions of Symmetry: Notebooks, Periodic Drawings and Related Work of M. C. Escher.* New York: W. H. Freeman, 1992.

Measurement

Eastman, P. D. *Big Dog…Little Dog*. New York: Random House, 1973.

Hutchins, Pat. *Happy Birthday Sam*. New York: Mulberry, 1991.

Keats, Ezra Jack. *Peter's Chair*. New York: HarperTrophy, 1967.

Lionni, Leo. *The Biggest House in the World*. New York: Alfred A Knopf, 1987.

Myller, Rolf. *How Big Is a Foot?* New York: Young Yearling, 1991.

Geometry

Ayres, Pam. *Guess Where*. Cambridge, MA: Candlewick Press, 1994.

Ashforth, Camilla. *Horatio's Bed*. Cambridge, MA: Candlewick Press, 1992.

Berenstain, Stan and Jan. *Inside, Outside, Upside Down*. New York: Random House, 1968.

Ehlert, Lois. *Color Zoo*. New York: HarperCollins, 1989.

Hoberman, Mary Ann. *A House Is a House for Me*. New York: Puffin Books, 1982.

Seuss, Dr. *The Shape of Me and Other Stuff*. New York: Beginner Books, 1973.

Poetry Anthologies

Blishen, Edward. *Oxford Book of Poetry for Children*. New York: Oxford University Press, 1987.

Cole, Joanna. *A New Treasury of Children's Poetry*. New York: Doubleday, 1984.

Prelutsky, Jack. *The Random House Book of Poetry for Children*. New York: Random House, 1983.

Stevenson, Robert Louis. *A Child's Garden of Verses*. New York: Delacorte, 1985.

Index of Math Concepts